A Year of Good Food:

Gourmet Cravings

- Lisa J. Locke -

CURRIES

**"Thou com'st in such a questionable shape
That I will speak to thee."**

Different modes of manufacture—The "native" fraud—"That man's family"—The French *kari*—A Parsee curry—"The oyster in the sauce"—Ingredients—Malay curry—Locusts—When to serve—What to curry—Prawn curry—Dry curry, a champion recipe—Rice—The Bombay duck.

The poor Indian grinds his coriander seeds, green ginger, and other ingredients between two large flat stones; taking a whiff at the family "hubble-bubble" pipe at intervals. The frugal British housewife purchases (alleged) curry powder in the warehouse of Italy—where it may have lived on, like Claudian, "through the centuries"—stirs a spoonful or two into the hashed mutton, surrounds it with a wall of clammy rice, and calls it BENARES CURRY, made from the recipe of a very dear uncle who met his death while tiger-shooting. And you will be in the minority if you do not cut this savoury meat with a knife, and eat potatoes, and very often cabbage, with it. The far-seeing eating-house keeper corrals a *Lascar* or a discharged *Mehtar* into the firm, gives him his board, a pound a month, and a clean *puggaree* and *Kummerbund* daily, and "stars" him in the bill as an "Indian *chef*, fresh from the Chowringhee Club, Calcutta." And it is part of the duties of this Oriental—supposed by the unwary to be at least a prince in his native land—to hand the portions of curry, which he may or may not have concocted, to the appreciative guests, who enjoy the repast all the more from having the scent of the Hooghly brought across the footlights. I was once sadly and solemnly reproved by the head waiter of a very "swagger" establishment indeed for sending away, after one little taste, the (alleged) curry which had been handed me by an exile from Ind, in snow-white raiment.

"You really ought to have eaten that, sir," said the waiter, "for that man's family have been celebrated curry-makers for generations."

I smole a broad smile. In the Land of the Moguls the very babies who roll in the dust know the secret of curry-making. But that "that man" had had any hand in the horrible concoction placed before me I still resolutely decline to believe. And how can a man be cook and waiter at the same time? The "native curry-maker," depend on it, is more or less of a fraud; and his aid is only invoked as an excuse for overcharging.

At the Oriental Club are served, or used to be served, really excellent curries, assorted; for as there be more ways than one of killing a cat, so are there more curries than one. The French turn out a horrible mixture, with parsley and mushrooms in it, which they call *kari*; it is called by a still worse name on the Boulevards, and the children of our lively neighbours are frequently threatened with it by their nurses.

On the whole, the East Indian method is the best; and the most philanthropic curry I ever tasted was one which my own *Khitmughar* had just prepared, with infinite pains, for his own consumption. The poor heathen had prospected a feast, as it was one of his numerous "big days"; so, despising the homely *dhal*, on the which, with a plate of rice and a modicum of rancid butter, he was wont to sustain existence, he had manufactured a savoury mess of pottage, the looks of which gratified me. So, at the risk of starting another Mutiny, it was ordained that the slave should serve the refection at the table of the "protector of the poor." And a *pukkha* curry it was, too. Another dish of native manufacture with which the writer became acquainted was a

Parsee Curry.

The eminent firm of Jehangeer on one occasion presented a petition to the commanding-officer that they might be allowed to supply a special curry to the mess one guest-night. The request was probably made as an inducement to some of the young officers to pay a little on account of their "owings" to the firm; but it is to be feared that no special vote of thanks followed the sampling of that special curry. It was a curry! I tasted it for a week (as the Frenchman did the soup of Swindon); and the Parsee *chef* must have upset the entire contents of the spice-box into it. I never felt more like murder than when the hotel cook in Manchester put nutmeg in the oyster sauce; but after that curry, the strangling of the entire firm of Jehangeer would, in our cantonments, at all events, have been brought in "justifiable homicide."

"Oyster sauce" recalls a quaint *simile* I once heard a bookmaker make use of. He was talking of one of his aristocratic debtors, whom he described as sure to pay up, if you could only get hold of him. "But mark you," continued the layer of odds, "he's just about as easy to get hold of as *the oyster in the sauce*, at one of our moonicipal banquets!" But return we to our coriander seeds. There is absolutely no reason why the frugal housewife in this country should not make her own curry powder from day to day, as it may be required. Here is an average Indian recipe; but it must be remembered that in the gorgeous East tastes vary as much as elsewhere, and that Bengal, Bombay, Madras (including Burmah), Ceylon, and the Straits Settlements, have all different methods of preparing a curry.

> A few coriander and cumin seeds—according to taste—eight peppercorns, a small piece of turmeric, and one dried chili, all pounded together.
>
> When making the curry *mixture*, take a piece of the heart of a cabbage, the size of a hen's egg; chop it fine and add one sour apple in thin slices the size of a Keswick codlin, the juice of a medium-sized lemon, a salt-spoonful of black pepper, and a tablespoonful of the above curry powder. Mix all well together; then take six medium-sized onions which have been chopped small and fried a delicate brown, a clove of garlic, also chopped small, two ounces of fresh butter, two ounces of flour, and one pint of beef gravy. Boil up this lot (which commences with the onions), and *when boiling* stir in the rest of the mixture. Let it all simmer down, and then add the solid part of the curry, *i.e.* the meat, cut in portions not larger than two inches square.

Remember, O frugal housewife, that the turmeric portion of the entertainment should be added with a niggard hand. "Too much turmeric" is the fault which is found with most curries made in England. I remember, when a boy, that there was an idea rooted in my mind that curries were made with Doctor Gregory's Powder, an unsavoury drug with which we were periodically regaled by the head nurse; and there was always a fierce conflict at the dinner-table when the bill-of-fare included this (as we supposed) physic-al terror. But it was simply the taste of turmeric to which we took exception.

What is Turmeric? A plant in cultivation all over India, whose tubers yield a deep yellow powder of a resinous nature. This resinous powder is sold in lumps, and is largely used for adulterating mustard; just as inferior anchovy sauce is principally composed of Armenian Bole, the deep red powder with which the actor makes up his countenance. Turmeric is also used medicinally in Hindustan, but not this side of Suez, although in chemistry it affords an infallible test for the presence of alkalies. The Coriander has become naturalised in parts of England, but is more used on the Continent. Our confectioners put the seeds in cakes and buns, also comfits, and in Germany, Norway, Sweden, and (I fancy) Russia, they figure in household bread. In the south of England, coriander and caraway seeds are sown side by side, and crops of each are obtained in alternate years. The coriander seed, too, is largely used with that of the caraway and the cumin, for making the liqueur known as Kümmel.

Cumin is mentioned in Scripture as something particularly nice. The seeds are sweet-savoured, something like those of the caraway, but more potent. In Germany they put them into bread, and the Dutch use them to flavour their cheeses. The seeds we get in England come principally from Sicily and Malta.

And now that my readers know all about the ingredients of curry-powder—it is assumed that no analysis of the chili, the ginger-root, or the peppercorn, is needed—let them emulate the pupils of Mr. Wackford Squeers, and "go and do it."

Another Recipe for curry-powder includes fenugreek, cardamoms, allspice, and cloves; but I verily believe that this was the powder used in that abominable Parsee hell-broth, above alluded to, so it should be cautiously approached, if at all. "Fenugreek" sounds evil; and I should say a curry compounded of the above ingredients would taste like a "Number One" pick-me-up. Yet another recipe (Doctor Kitchener's) specifies six ounces of coriander seed, five ounces of turmeric (*ower muckle, I'm of opeenion*) two ounces each of black pepper and mustard seed (*ochone!*), half an ounce of cumin seed, half an ounce of cinnamon (*donner und blitzen!*), and one ounce of lesser cardamoms. All these things are to be placed in a cool oven, kept therein one night, and pounded in a marble mortar next morning, preparatory to being rubbed through a sieve. "Kitchener" sounds like a good cooking name; but, with all due respect, I am not going to recommend his curry-powder.

A MALAY CURRY is made with blanched almonds, which should be fried in butter till lightly browned. Then pound them to a paste with a sliced onion and some thin lemon-rind. Curry powder and gravy are added, and a small quantity of cream. The Malays curry all sorts of fish, flesh, and fowl, including the young shoots of the bamboo—and nice tender, succulent morsels they are. At a hotel overlooking the harbour of Point de Galle, Ceylon, "run," at the time of the writer's visit, by a most convivial and enterprising Yankee, a canning concocter of all sorts of "slings" and "cocktails," there used to be quite a plethora of curries in the bill-of-fare. But for a prawn curry there is no place like the City of Palaces. And the reason for this super-excellence is that the prawns—but that story had, perhaps, best remain untold.

CURRIED LOCUSTS formed one of the most eccentric dishes ever tasted by the writer. There had come upon us that day a plague of these all-devouring insects. A few billions called on us, in our kitchen gardens, in passing; and whilst they ate up every green thing—including the newly-painted wheelbarrow, and the regimental standard, which had been incautiously left out of doors—our faithful blacks managed to capture several *impis* of the marauding scuts, in revenge; and the mess-cook made a right savoury *plât* of their hind-quarters.

It is criminal to serve curry during the *entrée* period of dinner. And it is worse form still to hand it round after gooseberry tart and cream, and trifle, as I have seen done at one great house. In the land of its birth, the spicy pottage invariably precedes the sweets. Nubbee Bux marches solemnly round with the mixture, in a deep dish, and is succeeded by Ram Lal with the rice. And in the Madras Presidency, where *dry* curry is served as well as the other brand, there is a procession of three brown attendants. Highly-seasoned dishes at the commencement of a long meal are a mistake; and this is one of the reasons why I prefer the middle cut of a plain-boiled Tay salmon, or the tit-bit of a lordly turbot, or a flake or two of a Grimsby cod, to a *sole Normande,* or a red mullet stewed with garlic, mushrooms, and inferior claret. I have even met *homard à l'Américaine,* during the fish course, at the special request of a well-known Duke. The soup, too, eaten at a large dinner should be as plain as possible; the edge being fairly taken off the appetite by such concoctions as *bisque, bouillabaisse,* and *mulligatawny*—all savoury and tasty dishes, but each a meal in itself. Then I maintain that to curry whitebait is wrong; partly because curry should on no account be served before roast and boiled, and partly because the flavour of the whitebait is too delicate for the fish to be clad in spices and onions. The lesson which all dinner-givers ought to have learnt from the Ancient Romans—the first people on record who went in for æsthetic cookery—is that highly-seasoned and well-peppered dishes should figure at the end, and not the commencement of a banquet. Here follows a list of some of the productions of Nature which it is allowable to curry.

What to Curry.

Turbot. Sole. Cod.

Lobster. Crayfish. Prawns,—but *not* the so-called "Dublin Prawn," which is delicious when eaten plain boiled, but no good in a curry.

Whelks.[6] Oysters. Scallops.

Mutton. Veal. Pork. Calf's Head. Ox Palate. Tripe.[6]

Eggs. Chicken. Rabbit (the "bunny" lends itself better than anything else to this method of cooking). Pease. Kidney Beans.[6] Vegetable Marrow. Carrots. Parsnips. Bamboo Shoots. Locust Legs.

A mistaken notion has prevailed for some time amongst men and women who write books, that the Indian curry mixture is almost red-hot to the taste. As a matter of fact it is of a far milder nature than many I have tasted "on this side." Also the Anglo-Indian does not sustain life entirely on food flavoured with turmeric and garlic. In fact, during a stay of seven years in the gorgeous East, the writer's experience was that not one in ten touched curry at the dinner table. At second breakfast—otherwise known as "tiffin"—it was a favoured dish; but the stuff prepared for the meal of the day—or the bulk thereof—usually went to gratify the voracious appetite of the "*mehters*," the Hindus who swept out the mess-rooms, and whose lowness of "caste" allowed them to eat "anything." An eccentric meal was the *mehter's* dinner. Into the empty preserved-meat tin which he brought round to the back door I have seen emptied such assorted *pabulum* as mock turtle soup, lobster salad, plum pudding and custard, curry, and (of course), the surplus *vilolif*; and in a few seconds he was squatting on his heels, and spading into the mixture with both hands.

In the Bengal Presidency cocoa-nut is freely used with a curry dressing; and as some men have as great a horror of this addition, as of oil in a salad, it is as well to consult the tastes of your guests beforehand.

A Prawn Curry I have seen made in Calcutta as follows, the proportions of spices, etc., being specially written down by a *munshi*:—

> Pound and mix one tablespoonful of coriander seed, one tablespoonful of poppy seed, a salt-spoonful of turmeric, half a salt-spoonful of cumin seed, a pinch of ground cinnamon, a ditto of ground nutmeg, a small lump of ginger, and one salt-spoonful of salt. Mix this with butter, add two sliced onions, and fry till lightly browned. Add the prawns, shelled, and pour in the milk of a cocoa-nut. Simmer for twenty minutes, and add some lime juice.

But the champion of curries ever sampled by the writer was a dry curry—a decided improvement on those usually served in the Madras Presidency—and the recipe (which has been already published in the *Sporting Times* and *Lady's Pictorial*), only came into the writer's possession some years after he had quitted the land of temples.

Dry Curry.

1 lb. of meat (mutton, fowl, or white fish).
1 lb. of onions.
1 clove of garlic.
2 ounces of butter.
1 dessert-spoonful of curry powder.
1 dessert-spoonful of curry paste.

> 1 dessert-spoonful of chutnee (or tamarind preserve, according to taste).

A very little cassareep, which is a condiment (only obtainable at a few London shops) made from the juice of the bitter cassava, or manioc root. Cassareep is the basis of that favourite West Indian dish "Pepper-pot."

> Salt to taste.
> A good squeeze of lemon juice.

First brown the onions in the butter, and then dry them. Add the garlic, which must be mashed to a pulp with the blade of a knife. Then mix the powder, paste, chutnee, and cassareep into a thin paste with the lemon juice. Mash the dried onions into this, and let all cook gently till thoroughly mixed. Then add the meat, cut into small cubes, and let all simmer very gently for three hours. This sounds a long time, but it must be remembered that the recipe is for a *dry* curry; and when served there should be no liquid about it.

'Tis a troublesome dish to prepare; but, judging from the flattering communications received by the writer, the lieges would seem to like it. And the mixture had better be cooked in a *double* or porridge-saucepan, to prevent any "catching."

Already, in one of the breakfast chapters, has the subject of the preparation of rice, to be served with curry, been touched upon; but there will be no harm done in giving the directions again.

Rice for Curry

Soak a sufficiency of rice in cold water until by repeated strainings all the dirt is separated from it. Then put the rice into *boiling* water, and let it "gallop" for nine or ten minutes—*no longer*. Strain the water off through a colander, and dash a little *cold* water over the rice to separate the grains. Put in a hot dish, and serve immediately.

A simple enough recipe, surely? So let us hear no more complaints of stodgy, clammy, "puddingy" rice. Most of the cookery books give far more elaborate directions, but the above is the method usually pursued by the poor brown heathen himself.

Soyer's recipe resembles the above; but, after draining the water from the cooked rice, it is replaced in the saucepan, the interior of which has in the interim been anointed with butter. The saucepan is then placed either near the fire (not on it), or in a slow oven, for the rice to swell.

Another way:

> After washing the rice, throw it into plenty of boiling water—in the proportion of six pints of water to one pound of rice. Boil it for five minutes, and skim it; then add a wine-glassful of milk for every half pound of rice, and continue boiling for five minutes longer. Strain the water off through a colander, and put it dry into the pot, on the corner of the stove, pouring over the rice a small piece of butter, which has been melted in a tablespoonful of the hot milk and water in which the rice was boiled. Add salt, and stir the rice for five minutes more.

The decayed denizen of the ocean, dried to the consistency of biscuit, and known in Hindustan as a BOMBAY DUCK, which is frequently eaten with curry, "over yonder," does not find much favour, this side of Port Said, although I have met the fowl in certain city restaurants. The addition is not looked upon with any particular favour by the writer.

"I have yet to learn" once observed that great and good man, the late Doctor Joseph Pope,[7] to the writer, in a discussion on "postponed" game, "that it is a good thing to put corruption into the human stomach."

SALADS

"O green and glorious, O herbaceous meat!
'Twould tempt the dying anchorite to eat.
Back to the world he'd turn his weary soul,
And dip his fingers in the salad bowl!"

Nebuchadnezzar *v.* Sydney Smith—Salt?—No salad-bowl—French origin—Apocryphal story of Francatelli—Salads *and* salads—Water-cress and dirty water—Salad-maker born not made—Lobster salad—Lettuce, Wipe or wash?—Mayonnaise—Potato salad—Tomato ditto—Celery ditto—A memorable ditto.

If Sydney Smith had only possessed the experience of old King Nebuchadnezzar, after he had been "turned out to grass," the witty prebend might not have waxed quite so enthusiastic on the subject of "herbaceous meat." Still the subject is a vast and important one, in its connection with gastronomy, and lends itself to poetry far easier than doth the little sucking pig, upon whom Charles Lamb expended so great and unnecessary a wealth of language.

But look at the terse, perfunctory, and far from satisfactory manner in which the *Encyclopædia* attacks the subject. "Salad," we read, "is the term given to a preparation of raw herbs for food. It derives its name from the fact that salt is one of the chief ingredients used in dressing a salad." This statement is not only misleading but startling; for in the "dressing" of a salad it would be the act of a lunatic to make salt the "chief ingredient."

Long before they had learnt the art of dressing the herbs, our ancestors partook of cresses (assorted), celery, and lettuces, after being soaked in water for a considerable period; and they dipped the raw herbs into salt before consuming them. In fact, in many a cheap eating-house of to-day, the term "salad" means plain lettuce, or cress, or possibly both, absolutely undressed—in a state of nature, *plus* plenty of dirty water. Even the English cook of the end of the nineteenth century cannot rid himself, or herself, of the idea that lettuce, like water-cress, knows the running brook, or the peaceful pond, as its natural element. And thirty years before the end of that century, a salad bowl was absolutely unknown in nine-tenths of the eating-houses of Great Britain.

There is no use in blinking the fact that it is to our lively neighbours that we owe the introduction of the salad proper. Often as the writer has been compelled, in these pages, to inveigh against the torturing of good fish and flesh by the alien cook, and the high prices charged for its endowment with an alien flavour, let that writer (figuratively) place a crown of endive, tipped with baby onions, upon the brows of the philanthropist who dressed the first salad, and gave the recipe to the world. That recipe has, of course, been improved upon; and although the *savant* who writes in the *Encyclopædia* proclaims that "salad has always been a favourite food with civilised nations, and has varied very little in its composition," the accuracy of both statements is open to question.

"Every art," observes another writer, "has its monstrosities; gastronomy has not been behind-hand; and though he must be a bold man who will venture to blaspheme the elegancies of French cookery, there comes a time to every Englishman who may have wandered into a mistaken admiration of sophisticated messes, when he longs for the simple diet of his native land, and vows that the best cookery in the world, and that which satisfies the most refined epicureanism, sets up for its ideal—plainness of good food, and the cultivation of natural tastes."

And yet the French have taught us, or tried to teach us, how to prepare a dish of raw herbs, in the simplest way in the world!

"Now a salad," says the same writer, "is simplicity itself, and here is a marvel—it is the crowning grace of a French dinner, while, on the other hand, it is little understood and villainously treated at English tables." Ahem! I would qualify that last statement. At *some* English tables I have tasted salads compared with which the happiest effort of the *chef* deserves not to be mentioned in the same garlic-laden breath. And "garlic-laden breath" naturally reminds me of the story of Francatelli—of which anecdote I do not believe one word, by the way. It was said of Franc., whilst *chef* at the Reform Club, that his salads were such masterpieces, such things of beauty, that one of the members questioned him on the subject.

"How do you manage to introduce such a delicious flavour into your salads?"

"Ah! that should be my secret," was the reply. "But I will tell him to you. After I have made all my preparations, and the green food is mixed with the dressing, I chew a little clove of garlic between my teeth—so—and then breathe gently over the whole."

But, as observed before, I do not believe that garlic story.

O salad, what monstrosities are perpetrated in thy name! Let the genteel boarding-house cook-maid, the young lady who has studied harmony and the higher mathematics at the Board School, spread herself over the subject; and then invite the angels to inspect the matter, and weep! For this is the sort of "harmony" which the "paying guest," who can appreciate the advantages of young and musical society, an airy front bed-chamber, and a bicycle room, is expected to enthuse over at the *table d'hôte*: a *mélange* of herbs and roots, including water-cress and giant radishes, swimming in equal parts of vinegar and oil, and a large proportion of the water in which the ingredients have been soaking for hours—said ingredients being minced small, like veal collops, with a steel knife. And the same salad, the very identical horror, obtrudes itself on the table at other genteel establishments than boarding-houses. For they be "mostly fools" who people the civilised world.

Let it be laid down as a golden rule, that the concoction of a salad should never, or hardly ever, be entrusted to the tender mercies of the British serving-maid. For the salad-maker, like the poet, is born, not made; and the divine *afflatus*—I don't mean garlic—is as essential in the one as in the other. We will take the simple mixture, what is commonly known as the

French Salad,

first. This is either composed, in the matter of herbs, of lettuce, chopped taragon, chervil, and chives; or of endive, with, "lurking in the bowl," a *chapon*, or crust of bread on which a clove of garlic has been rubbed. But the waiter, an he be discreet, will ask the customer beforehand if he prefer that the *chapon* be omitted. The dressing is simplicity itself:

> Within the bowl of a table-spoon are placed, in succession, a spot of made mustard, and a sprinkling of black pepper and salt. The bowl is filled up with vinegar, and with a fork in the other hand the waiter stirs quickly the mustard, etc., afterwards emptying the contents of the spoon over the green-stuff. Then the spoon is refilled—either twice or thrice, *ad lib.*—with Lucca oil, which is also poured over the salad. Then the final mixing takes place, in the salad bowl.

But there be many and elaborate ways of salad-making. Here is the writer's idea of a

Lobster Salad

for half-a-dozen guests:

> In a soup plate, mix the yolks of two hard-boiled eggs—boiled for thirty minutes, and afterwards thrown into cold water—into a smooth paste with a teaspoonful of made mustard, and a tablespoonful of plain vinegar, added drop by drop. Keep on stirring, and add a dessert-spoonful of tarragon vinegar, a few drops of essence of anchovies, a teaspoonful (*not heaped*) of salt, about the same quantity of sifted sugar, and a good pinch of cayenne. [The tendency of black pepper is to make a salad gritty, which is an abomination.] Lastly, add, drop by drop, three tablespoonfuls of oil. Pour this dressing (which should be in a continual state of stir) into your salad bowl. Add the pickings of a hen lobster cut into dice, and atop of the lobster, lettuces which have been shred with clean fingers, or with ivory forks; a little endive may be added, with a slice or two of beetroot; but no onion (or very little) in a lobster salad. A few shreds of anchovy may be placed atop; with beetroot cut into shapes, the whites of the eggs, and the coral of the lobster, for the sake of effect; but seek not, O student, to achieve prettiness of effect to the detriment of practical utility. I need hardly add that the sooner after its manufacture a salad is eaten, the better will be its flavour. And the solid ingredients should only be mixed with the

dressing at the very last moment; otherwise a sodden, flabby effect will be produced, which is neither pleasing to the eye, nor calculated to promote good digestion.

I am perfectly aware that the above is not a strict *Mayonnaise* dressing, in which the egg yolks should be raw, instead of cooked. But, like the Scotsman, I have "tried baith," and prefer my own way, which more resembles the *sauce Tartare*, than the *Mayonnaise* of our lively neighbours, who, by the way, merely wipe, instead of wash, their lettuces and endive, to preserve, as they say, the flavour. Of course this is a matter of taste, but the writer must own to a preference for the baptised article, which must, however, on no account be left to soak, but be simply freed from dirt, grit, and—other things.

What is the origin of the word "MAYONNAISE"? No two Frenchmen will give you the same answer. "Of or belonging to Mayonne" would seem to be the meaning of the word; but then there is no such place as Mayonne in the whole of France. Grimod de la Reyniere maintained that the proper word was "BAYONNAISE," meaning a native of Bayonne, on the Spanish frontier. Afterwards Grimod, who was a resourceful man, got hold of another idea, and said that the word was probably "MAHONNAISE," and so named in honour of Marshal Richelieu's capture of the stronghold of Mahon, in the island of Minorca. But what had this victory got to do with a salad dressing? What was the connection of raw eggs and tarragon vinegar with Marshal Richelieu? Then up came another cook, in the person of Carême, who established it as an absolute certainty that the genuine word was "MAGNONNAISE," from the word "*manier*," to manipulate. But as nobody would stand this definition for long, a fresh search had to be made; and this time an old Provençal verb was dug up—*mahonner*, or more correctly *maghonner*, to worry or fatigue. And this is now said by purists to be the source of *Mayonnaise*—"something worried," or fatigued. And the reason for the gender of the noun is said to be that in ancient times lovely woman was accustomed to manipulate the salad with her own fair fingers. In the time of Rousseau, the phrase *retourner la salade avec les doigts* was used to describe a woman as being still young and beautiful; just as in Yorkshire at the present time, "she canna mak' a bit o' bread" is used to describe a woman who is of no possible use in the house. So a *Mayonnaise* or a *Mahonnaise*—I care not which be the correct spelling—was a young lady who "fatigued" the salad. More shame to the gallants of the day, who allowed "fatigue" to be associated with youth and beauty!

But can it possibly matter what the word means, when the mixture is smooth and savoury; and so deftly blended that no one flavour predominates? And herein lies the secret of every mixture used for the refreshment of the inner man and woman; whether it be a soup, a curry, a trifle, a punch, or a cup—no one ingredient should be of more weight or importance than another. And that was the secret of the "delicious gravy" furnished by the celebrated stew at the "Jolly Farmers," in *The Old Curiosity Shop* of Charles Dickens.

Mayonnaise (we will drop for the nonce, the other spelling) is made thus:

> In the proportions of two egg yolks to half a pint of Lucca oil, and a small wine-glassful of tarragon vinegar. Work the yolks smooth in a basin, with a seasoning of pepper (cayenne for choice), salt, and—according to the writer's views—sifted sugar. Then a few drops of oil, and fewer of vinegar; stirring the mixture all the time, from right to left, with a wooden, or ivory, spoon. In good truth 'tis a "fatiguing" task; and as in very hot weather the sauce is liable to decompose, or "curdle," before the finishing touches are put to it, it may be made over ice.

> "Stir, sisters, stir,
> Stir with care!"

is the motto for the *Mayonnaise*-mixer. And in many cases her only reward consists in the knowledge that through her art and patience she has helped to make the sojourn of others in this vale of tears less tearful and monotonous.

"Onion atoms" should "lurk within the bowl," on nearly every occasion, and as for a potato salad—don't be afraid, I'm not going to quote any more Sydney Smith, so don't get loading your guns—well, here is the proper way to make it.

Potato Salad.

Cut nine or ten average-sized kidney potatoes (cooked) into slices, half an inch thick, put them in a salad bowl, and pour over them, after mixing, two tablespoonfuls of vinegar, one tablespoonful of tarragon vinegar, six tablespoonfuls of oil, one of minced parsley, a dessert-spoonful of onions chopped very fine, with cayenne and salt to taste. Shredded anchovies may be added, although it is preferable without; and this salad should be made a couple of hours or so before partaken of.

The German recipe for a potato salad is too nasty to quote; and their HERRING SALAD, although said to be a valuable restorative of nerve power, by no means presents an attractive appearance, when served at table. Far more to the mind and palate of the average epicure is a

Tomato Salad.

This is the author's recipe:

Four large tomatoes and one Spanish onion, cut into thin slices. Mix a spot of mustard, a little white pepper and salt, with vinegar, in a tablespoon, pour it over the love apples, etc., and then add two tablespoonfuls of oil. Mix well, and then sprinkle over the mixture a few drops of Lea and Perrins's Worcester Sauce. For the fair sex, the last part of the programme may be omitted, but on no account leave out the breath of sunny Spain. And mark this well. The man, or woman, who mixes tomatoes with lettuces, or endives, in the bowl, is hereby sentenced to translate the whole of this book into Court English.

Celery Salad.

An excellent winter salad is made with beetroot and celery, cut in thin slices, and served—with or without onions—either with a mayonnaise sauce, or with a plain cream sauce: to every tablespoonful of cream add a teaspoonful of tarragon vinegar, a little sugar, and a suspicion of cayenne. This salad looks best served in alternate slices of beet and celery, on a flat silver dish, around the sauce.

A Gentleman Salad Maker.

Although in the metropolis it is still customary, in middle-class households, to hire "outside help" on the occasion of a dinner-party, we have not heard for some time of a salad-dresser who makes house-to-house visitations in the exercise of his profession. But, at the end of the 18th century, the Chevalier d'Allignac, who had escaped from Paris to London in the evil days of the Revolution, made a fortune in this way. He was paid at the rate of £5 a salad, and naturally, soon started his own carriage, "in order that he might pass quickly from house to house, during the dining hours of the aristocracy." High as the fee may appear to be, it is impossible to measure the width of the gulf which lies between the salad as made by a lover of the art, and the kitchen-wench; and a perfect salad is, like a perfect curry, "far above rubies."

A Memorable Salad

was once served in my own mansion. The *chef*, who understood these matters well, when her hair was free from vine leaves, had been celebrating her birthday or some other festival; and had mixed the dressing with Colza oil. Her funeral was largely attended.

SALADS AND CONDIMENTS

"Epicurean cooks
Sharpen with cloyless sauce his appetite."

Roman salad—Italian ditto—Various other salads—Sauce for cold mutton—Chutnine—Raw chutnee—Horse-radish sauce—Christopher North's sauce—How to serve a mackerel—*Sauce Tartare*—Ditto for sucking pig—Delights of making *Sambal*—A new language.

It has, I hope, been made sufficiently clear that neither water-cress nor radishes should figure in a dressed salad; from the which I would also exclude such "small deer" as mustard and cress. There is, however, no black mark against the narrow-leaved CORN SALAD plant, or "lamb's lettuce"; and its great advantage is that it can be grown almost anywhere during the winter months, when lettuces have to be "coddled," and thereby robbed of most of their flavour.

Instead of yolk of egg, in a dressing, cheese may be used, with good results, either cream cheese—*not* the poor stuff made on straws, but what are known as "napkin," or "New Forest" cheeses—or Cheddar. Squash it well up with oil and vinegar, and do not use too much. A piece of cheese the size of an average lump of sugar will be ample, and will lend a most agreeable flavour to the mixture.

Roman Salad

Lucullus and Co.—or rather their cooks—had much to learn in the preparation of the "herbaceous meat" which delighted Sydney Smith. The Romans cultivated endive; this was washed free from "matter in the wrong place," chopped small—absolutely fatal to the taste—anointed with oil and *liquamen*, topped up with chopped onions, and further ornamented with honey and vinegar. But before finding fault with the conquerors of the world for mixing honey with a salad, it should be remembered that they knew not "fine Demerara," nor "best lump," nor even the beet sugar which can be made at home. Still I should not set a Roman salad before my creditors, if I wanted them to have "patience." An offer of the very smallest dividend would be preferable.

Italian Salad.

The merry Italian has improved considerably upon the herbaceous treat (I rather prefer "treat" to "meat") of his ancestors; though he is far too fond of mixing flesh-meat of all sorts with his dressed herbs, and his boiled vegetables. Two cold potatoes and half a medium sized beet sliced, mixed with boiled celery and Brussels sprouts, form a common salad in the sunny South; the dressing being usually oil and vinegar, occasionally oil *seule*, and sometimes a *Tartare* sauce. Stoned olives are usually placed atop of the mess, which includes fragments of chicken, or veal and ham.

Russian Salad.

This is a difficult task to build up; for a sort of Cleopatra's Needle, or pyramid, of cooked vegetables, herbs, pickles, etc., has to be erected on a flat dish. Carrots, turnips, green peas, asparagus, French beans, beetroot, capers, pickled cucumbers, and horse-radish, form the solid matter of which the pyramid is built.

> Lay a *stratum* on the dish, and anoint the *stratum* with *Tartare* sauce. Each layer must be similarly anointed, and must be of less circumference than the one underneath, till the top layer consists of one caper. Garnish with bombs of caviare, sliced lemon, crayfish, olives, and salted cucumber; and then give the salad to the policeman on fixed-point duty. At least, if you take my advice.

Anchovy Salad.

This is usually eaten at the commencement of dinner, as a *hors d'œuvre*.

Some shreds of anchovy should be arranged "criss-cross" in a flat glass dish. Surround it with small heaps of chopped truffles, yolk and white of hard-boiled eggs, capers, and a stoned olive or two. Mix all the ingredients together with a little Chili vinegar, and twice the quantity of oil.

The mixture is said to be invaluable as an appetiser; but the modest oyster on the *deep shell*—if he has not been fattened at the bolt-hole of the main sewer—is to be preferred.

Cooked vegetables, for salad purposes, are not, nor will they ever be, popular in England, Nine out of ten Britains will eat the "one sauce" with asparagus, in preference to the oiled butter, or plain salad dressing, of mustard, vinegar, pepper, salt, and oil; whilst 'tis almost hopeless to attempt to dissuade madame the cook from smothering her cauliflowers with liquefied paste, before sending them to table. Many a wild weed which foreign nations snatch greedily from the soil, prior to dressing it, is passed by with scorn by our islanders, including the dandelion, which is a favourite of our lively neighbours, for salad purposes, and is doubtless highly beneficial to the human liver. So is the cauliflower; and an eminent medical authority once gave out that the man who ate a parboiled cauliflower, as a salad, every other day, need never send for a doctor. Which sounds rather like fouling his own nest.

Fruit Salad.

This is simply a French *compôte* of cherries, green almonds, pears, limes, peaches, apricots in syrup slightly flavoured with ginger; and goes excellent well with any cold brown game. Try it.

Orange Salad.

Peel your orange, and cut it into thin slices. Arrange these in a glass dish, and sugar them well. Then pour over them a glass of sherry, a glass of brandy, and a glass of maraschino.

Orange Sauce.

Cold mutton, according to my notions, is "absolutely beastly," to the palate. More happy homes have been broken up by this simple dish than by the entire army of Europe. And 'tis a dish which should never be allowed to wander outside the servants' hall. The superior domestics who take their meals in the steward's room, would certainly rise in a body, and protest against the indignity of a cold leg, or shoulder. As for a cold loin—but the idea is too awful. Still, brightened up by the following condiment, cold mutton will go down smoothly, and even gratefully:—

> Rub off the thin yellow rind of two oranges on four lumps of sugar. Put these into a bowl, and pour in a wine-glass of port, a quarter pint of dissolved red-currant jelly, a teaspoonful of mixed mustard—don't be frightened, it's all right—a finely-minced shallot, a pinch of cayenne, and some more thin orange rind. Mix well. When heated up, strain and bottle off.

But amateur sauces should, on the whole, be discouraged. The writer has tasted dozens of imitations of Lea and Perrins's "inimitable," and it is still inimitable, and unapproachable. It is the same with chutnee. You can get anything in that line you want at Stembridge's, close to Leicester Square, to whom the writer is indebted for some valuable hints. But here is a recipe for a mixture of chutnee and pickle, which must have been written a long time ago; for the two operations are transposed. For instance, *the onions should be dealt with first.*

Chutnine.

> Ten or twelve large apples, peeled and cored, put in an earthenware jar, with a little vinegar (on no account use water) in the oven. Let them remain till in a pulp, then take out, and add half an ounce of curry powder, one ounce of ground ginger, half a pound of stoned raisins, chopped fine, half a pound moist sugar, one teaspoonful cayenne pepper, one tablespoonful salt. Take four large onions (*this should be done first*), chop very fine, and put them in a jar with a pint and a half of vinegar. Cork tightly and let them remain a week. Then add the rest of the ingredients, after mixing them well together. Cork tightly, and

the chutnine will be ready for use in a month. It improves, however, by keeping for a year or so.

Raw Chutnee

is another aid to the consumption of cold meat, and I have also seen it used as an accompaniment to curry, but do not recommend the mixture.

One large tomato, one smaller Spanish onion, one green chili, and a squeeze of lemon juice. Pulp the tomato; don't try to extract the seeds, for life is too short for that operation. Chop the onion and the chili very fine, and mix the lot up with a pinch of salt, and the same quantity of sifted sugar.

I know plenty of men who would break up their homes (after serving the furniture in the same way) and emigrate; who would go on strike, were roast beef to be served at the dinner-table unaccompanied by horse-radish sauce. But this is a relish for the national dish which is frequently overlooked.

Horse-radish Sauce.

Grate a young root as fine as you can. It is perhaps needless to add that the fresher the horse-radish the better. No vegetables taste as well as those grown in your own garden, and gathered, or dug up, just before wanted. And the horse-radish, like the Jerusalem artichoke, comes to stay. When once he gets a footing in your garden you will never dislodge him; nor will you want to. Very well, then:

Having grated your horse, add a quarter of a pint of cream—English or Devonshire—a dessert-spoonful of sifted sugar, half that quantity of salt, and a tablespoonful of vinegar. Mix all together, and, if for hot meat, heat in the oven, taking care that the mixture does not curdle. Many people use oil instead of cream, and mix grated orange rind with the sauce. The Germans do not use oil, but either make the relish with cream, or hard-boiled yolk of egg. Horse-radish sauce for hot meat may also be heated by pouring it into a jar, and standing the jar in boiling water—"jugging it" in fact.

Celery Sauce,

for boiled pheasant, or turkey, is made thus:

Two or three heads of celery, sliced thin, put into a saucepan with equal quantities of sugar and salt, a dust of white pepper, and two or three ounces of butter. Stew your celery slowly till it becomes pulpy, but *not brown*, add two or three ounces of flour, and a good half-pint of milk, or cream. Let it simmer twenty minutes, and then rub the mixture through a sieve.

The carp as an item of food is, according to my ideas, a fraud. He tastes principally of the mud in which he has been wallowing until dragged out by the angler. The ancients loved a dish of carp, and yet they knew not the only sauce to make him at all palatable.

Sauce for Carp.

One ounce of butter, a quarter pint of good beef gravy, one dessert-spoonful of flour, a quarter pint of cream and two anchovies chopped very small. Mix over the fire, stir well till boiling, then take off, add a little Worcester sauce, and a squeeze of lemon, just before serving.

Christopher North's Sauce.

This is a very old recipe. Put a dessert-spoonful of sifted sugar, a salt-spoonful of salt, and rather more than that quantity of cayenne, into a jar. Mix thoroughly, and add, gradually, two tablespoonfuls of Harvey's sauce, a dessert-spoonful of mushroom ketchup, a tablespoonful of lemon juice, and a large glass of port. Place the jar in a saucepan of boiling water, and let it remain till the mixture is very hot, but not boiling. If bottled directly after made, the sauce will keep for a week, and may be used for duck, goose, pork, or (Christopher adds) "any broil." But there is but *one* broil sauce, the Gubbins Sauce, already mentioned in this work.

Sauce for Hare.

What a piece of work is a hare! And what a piece of work it is to cook him in a laudable fashion!

> Crumble some bread—a handful or so—soak it in port wine, heat over the fire with a small lump of butter, a tablespoonful of red-currant jelly, a little salt, and a tablespoonful of Chili vinegar. Serve as hot as possible.

Mackerel is a fish but seldom seen at the tables of the great. And yet 'tis tasty eating, if his Joseph's coat be bright and shining when you purchase him. When stale he is dangerous to life itself. And he prefers to gratify the human palate when accompanied by

Gooseberry Sauce,

which is made by simply boiling a few green gooseberries, rubbing them through a sieve, and adding a little butter and a suspicion of ginger. Then heat up. "A wine-glassful of sorrel or spinach-juice," observes one authority, "is a decided improvement." H'm. I've tried both, and prefer the gooseberries unadorned with spinach liquor.

Now for a sauce which is deservedly popular all over the world, and which is equally at home as a salad dressing, as a covering for a steak off a fresh-run salmon, or a portion of fried eel; the luscious, the invigorating

Sauce Tartare,

so called because no tallow-eating Tartar was ever known to taste thereof. I have already given a pretty good recipe for its manufacture, in previous salad-dressing instructions, where the yolks of hard-boiled eggs are used. But chopped chervil, shallots, and (occasionally) gherkins, are added to the

Tartare arrangement; and frequently the surface is adorned with capers, stoned olives, and shredded anchovies.

In the chapters devoted to dinners, no mention has been made of the sucking pig, beloved of Charles Lamb.[8] This hardened offender should be devoured with

Currant Sauce:

> Boil an ounce of currants, after washing them and picking out the tacks, dead flies, etc., in half a pint of water, for a few minutes, and pour over them a cupful of finely grated crumbs. Let them soak well, then beat up with a fork, and stir in about a gill of oiled butter. Add two tablespoonfuls of the brown gravy made for the pig, a glass of port, and a pinch of salt. Stir the sauce well over the fire. It is also occasionally served with roast venison; but not in the mansions of my friends.

What is sauce for Madame Goose is said to be sauce for Old Man Gander. Never mind about that, however. The parents of young Master Goose, with whom alone I am going to deal, have, like the flowers which bloom in the spring, absolutely nothing to do with the case. This is the best

Sauce for the Goose

known to civilisation:

> Put two ounces of green sage leaves into a jar with an ounce of the thin yellow rind of a lemon, a minced shallot, a teaspoonful of salt, half a ditto of cayenne, and a pint of claret. Let this soak for a fortnight, then pour off the liquid into a tureen; or boil with some good gravy. This sauce will keep for a week or two, bottled and well corked up.

And now, having given directions for the manufacture of sundry "cloyless sauces"—with only one of the number having any connection with *Ala*, and that one a sauce of world-wide reputation, I will conclude this chapter with a little fancy work. It is not probable that many who do me the honour to skim through these humble, faultily-written, but heartfelt gastronomic hints are personally acquainted with the cloyless

Sambal,

who is a lady of dusky origin. But let us quit metaphor, and direct the gardener to

> Cut the finest and straightest cucumber in his crystal palace. Cut both ends off, and divide the remainder into two-inch lengths. Peel these, and let them repose in salt to draw out the water, which is the indigestible part of the cucumber. Then take each length, in succession, and with a very sharp knife—a penknife is best for the purpose—pare it from surface to centre, until it has become one long, curly shred. Curl it up tight, so that it may resemble in form the spring of a Waterbury watch. Cut the length through from end to end, until you have made numerous long thin shreds. Treat each length in the same way, and place in a glass dish. Add three green chilies, chopped fine, a few chopped spring onions, and some tiny shreds of the Blue Fish of Java. Having performed a fishless pilgrimage in search of this curiosity, you will naturally fall back upon the common or Italian anchovy, which, after extracting the brine and bones, and cleansing, chop fine. Pour a little vinegar over the mixture.

"Sambal" will be found a delicious accompaniment to curry—when served on a salad plate—or to almost any description of cold meat and cheese. It is only fair to add, however, that the task of making the relish is arduous and exasperating to a degree; and that the woman who makes it—no male Christian in the world is possessed of a tithe of the necessary patience, now that Job and Robert Bruce are no more—should have the apartment to herself. For the labour is calculated to teach an entirely new language to the manufacturer.

SUPPER

"We are such stuff
As dreams are made of."

Cleopatra's supper—Oysters—Danger in the Aden bivalve—Oyster stew—Ball suppers—Pretty dishes—The *Taj Mahal*—Aspic—Bloater paste and whipped cream—Ladies' recipes—Cookery colleges—Tripe—Smothered in onions—North Riding fashion—An hotel supper—Lord Tomnoddy at the "Magpie and Stump."

That cruel and catlike courtesan, Cleopatra, is alleged to have given the most expensive supper on record, and to have disposed of the *bonne bouche* herself, in the shape of a pearl, valued at the equivalent of £250,000, dissolved in vinegar of extra strength. Such a sum is rather more than is paid for a supper at the Savoy, or the Cecil, or the Metropole, in these more practical times, when pearls are to be had cheaper; and there is probably about as much truth in this pearl story as in a great many others of the same period. I have heard of a fair *declassée* leader of fashion at Monte Carlo, who commanded that her *major domo* should be put to death for not having telegraphed to Paris for peaches, for a special dinner; but the woman who could melt a pearl in vinegar, and then drink——*halte la!* Perhaps the pearl was displayed in the deep shell of the oyster of which the "noble curtesan" partook? We know how Mark Antony's countrymen valued the succulent bivalve; and probably an oyster feast at Wady Halfa or Dongola was a common function long before London knew a "Scott's," a "Pimm's," or a "Sweeting's."

Thanks partly to the "typhoid scare," but principally to the prohibitive price, the "native" industry of Britain has been, at the latter end of the nineteenth century, by no means active, although in the illustrated annuals Uncle John still brings with him a barrel of the luscious bivalves, in addition to assorted toys for the children, when he arrives in the midst of a snow-storm at the old hall on Christmas Eve. But Uncle John, that good fairy of our youth, when Charles Dickens invented the "festive season," and the very atmosphere reeked of goose-stuffing, resides, for the most part, "in Sheffield," in these practical days, when sentiment and goodwill to relatives are rapidly giving place to matters of fact, motor cars, and mammoth rates.

The Asiatic oyster is not altogether commendable, his chief merit consisting in his size. Once whilst paying a flying visit to the city of Kurachi, I ordered a dozen oysters at the principal hotel. Then I went out to inspect the lions. On my return I could hardly push my way into the coffee-room. It was full of oyster! There was no room for anything else. In fact *one* Kurachi oyster is a meal for four full-grown men.

More tragic still was my experience of the bivalves procurable at Aden—which cinder-heap I have always considered to be a foretaste of even hotter things below. Instead of living on coal-dust (as might naturally be expected) the Aden oyster appears to do himself particularly well on some preparation of copper. The only time I tasted him, the after consequences very nearly prevented my ever tasting anything else, on this sphere. And it was only the comfort administered by the steward of my cabin which got me round.

"Ah!" said that functionary, as he looked in to see whether I would take hot pickled pork or roast goose for dinner. "The last time we touched at Aden, there was two gents 'ad 'ysters. One of 'em died the same night, and the other nex' mornin'."

I laughed so much that the poison left my system.

Yet still we eat oysters—the *Sans Bacilles* brand, for choice. And if we can only persuade the young gentleman who opens the bivalves to refrain from washing the grit off each in the tub of dirty water behind the bar, so much the better. And above all, the bivalves should be opened on the *deep* shell, so as to conserve some of the juice; for it is advisable to get as much of the bivalve as we can for the money. Every time I crunch the bones of a lark I feel that I am devouring an oratorio, in the way of song; and whilst the bivalve is sliding down the "red lane" it may be as well to reflect that "there slips away fourpence"; or, as the Scotsman had it, "bang went saxpence!"

In connection with Mr. Bob Sawyer's supper party in *Pickwick*, it may be recollected that "the man to whom the order for the oysters had been sent had not been told to open them; it is a very difficult thing to open an oyster with a limp knife or a two-pronged fork: and very little was done in this way."

And in one's own house, unless there be an adept at oyster-opening present, the simplest way to treat the bivalve is the following. It should be remembered that a badly-opened oyster will resemble in flavour a slug on a gravel walk. So *roast* him, good friends, in his own fortress.

Oysters in their own Juice.

With the tongs place half-a-dozen oysters, mouths outwards, between the red-hot coals of the parlour or dining-room fire—the deep shell must be at the bottom—and the oysters will be cooked in a few minutes, or when the shells gape wide. Pull them out with the tongs, and insert a fresh batch. No pepper, vinegar, or lemon juice is necessary as an adjunct; and the oyster never tastes better.

At most eating-houses,

Scalloped Oysters

taste of nothing but scorched bread-crumbs; and the reason is obvious, for there is but little else in the scallop shell. *Natives only* should be used.

Open and beard two dozen, and cut each bivalve in half. Melt two ounces of butter in a stewpan, and mix into it the same allowance of flour, the strained oyster liquor, a teacupful of cream, half a teaspoonful of essence of anchovies, and a pinch of cayenne—death to the caitiff who adds nutmeg—and stir the sauce well over the fire. Take it off, and add the well-beaten yolks of two eggs, a tablespoonful of finely chopped parsley, and a teaspoonful of lemon juice. Put in the oysters, and stir the whole over a gentle fire for five minutes. Put the mixture in the shells, grate bread-crumbs over, place a small piece of butter atop, and bake in a Dutch oven before a clear fire until the crumbs are lightly browned, which should be in about a quarter of an hour.

Oyster Stew

is thoroughly understood in New York City. On this side, the dish does not meet with any particular favour, although no supper-table is properly furnished without it.

> Open two dozen oysters, and take the beards off. Put the oysters into a basin and squeeze over them the juice of half a lemon. Put the beards and the strained liquor into a saucepan with half a blade of mace, half a dozen peppercorns ground, a little grated lemon rind, and a pinch of cayenne. Simmer gently for a quarter of an hour, strain the liquid, thicken it with a little butter and flour, add a quarter of a pint (or a teacupful) of cream, and stir over the fire till quite smooth. Then put in the oysters, and let them warm through—they must not boil. Serve in a soup tureen, and little cubes of bread fried in bacon grease may be served with the stew, as with pea-soup.

Be very careful to whose care you entrust your barrel, or bag, of oysters, after you have got them home. A consignment of the writer's were, on one memorable and bitter cold Christmas Eve, consigned to the back dairy, by Matilda Anne. Result—frostbite, gapes, dissolution, disappointment, disagreeable language.

Ball Suppers.

More hard cash is wasted on these than even on ball dresses, which is saying a great deal. The alien caterer, or *charcutier*, is chiefly to blame for this; for he it is who has taught the British matron to wrap up wholesome food in coats of grease, inlaid with foreign substances, to destroy its flavour, and to bestow upon it an outward semblance other than its own. There was handed unto me, only the other evening, what I at first imagined to be a small section of the celebrated *Taj Mahal* at Agra, the magnificent mausoleum of the Emperor Shah Jehan. Reference to the bill-of-fare established the fact that I was merely sampling a galantine of turkey, smothered in some white glazy grease, inlaid with chopped carrot, green peas, truffles, and other things. And the marble column (also inlaid) which might have belonged to King Solomon's Temple, at the top of the table, turned out to be a Tay salmon, decorated *à la mode de charcutier*, and tasting principally of garlic. A shriek from a fair neighbour caused me to turn my head in her direction; and it took some little time to discover, and to convince her, that the item on her plate was not a mouse, too frightened to move, but some preparation of the liver of a goose, in "aspic."

This said Aspic—which has no connection with the asp which the fair Cleopatra kept on the premises, although a great French lexicographer says that aspic is so called because it is as cold as a snake—is invaluable in the numerous "schools of cookery" in the which British females are educated according to the teaching of the bad fairy *Ala*. The cold chicken and ham which delighted our ancestors at the supper-table—what has become of them? Yonder, my dear sir, is the fowl, in neat portions, minced, and made to represent fragments of the almond rock which delighted us whilst in the nursery. The ham has become a ridiculous *mousse*, placed in little accordion-pleated receptacles of snow-white paper; and those are not poached eggs atop, either, but dabs of whipped cream with a preserved apricot in the centre.

It was only the other day that I read in a journal written by ladies for ladies, of a dainty dish for luncheon or supper: *croûtons* smeared with bloater paste and surmounted with whipped cream; and in the same paper was a recipe for stuffing a fresh herring with mushrooms, parsley, yolk of egg, onion, and its own soft roe. I am of opinion that it was a bad day for the male Briton when the gudewife, with her gude-daughter, and her gude cook, abandoned the gude roast and boiled, in favour of the works of the all-powerful *Ala*.

And now let us proceed to discuss the most homely supper of all, and when I mention the magic word

Tripe

there be few of my readers who will not at once allow that it is not only the most homely of food, but forms an ideal supper. This doctrine had not got in its work, however, in the 'sixties, at about which period the man who avowed himself an habitual tripe-eater must have been possessed of a considerable amount of nerve. Some of the supper-houses served it—such as the Albion, the Coal Hole, and more particularly, "Noakes's," the familiar name for the old Opera Tavern which used to face the Royal Italian Opera House, in Bow Street, Covent Garden. But the more genteel food-emporiums fought shy of tripe until within three decades of the close of the nineteenth century. Then it began to figure on the supper bills, in out-of-the-way corners; until supper-eaters in general discovered that this was not only an exceedingly cheap, but a very nourishing article of food, which did not require any special divine aid to digest. Then the price of tripe went up 75 per cent on the programmes. Then the most popular burlesque *artiste* of any age put the stamp of approval upon the new supper-dish, and tripe-dressing became as lucrative a profession as gold-crushing.

There is a legend afloat of an eminent actor—poor "Ned" Sothern, I fancy, as "Johnny" Toole would never have done such a thing—who bade some of his friends and acquaintance to supper, and regaled them on sundry rolls of house flannel, smothered with the orthodox onion sauce. But that is another story. Practical jokes should find no place in this volume, which is written to benefit, and not alarm, posterity. Therefore let us discuss the problem

How to Cook Tripe.

Ask for "double-tripe," and see that the dresser gives it you nice and white. Wash it, cut into portions, and place in equal parts of milk and water, boiling fast. Remove the saucepan from the hottest part of the fire, and let the tripe keep just on the boil for an hour and a half. Serve with whole onions and onion sauce—in this work you will not be told how to manufacture onion sauce—and baked potatoes should always accompany this dish to table.

Some people like their tripe cut into strips rolled up and tied with cotton, before being placed in the saucepan; but there is really no necessity to take this further trouble. And if the cook should forget to remove the cotton before serving, you might get your tongues tied in knots. In the North Riding of Yorkshire, some of the farmers' wives egg-and-bread-crumb fillets of tripe, and fry them in the drip of thick rashers of ham which have been fried previously. The ham is served in the centre of the dish, with the fillets around the pig-pieces. This is said to be an excellent dish, but I prefer my tripe smothered in onions, like the timid "bunny."

Edmund Yates, in his "Reminiscences," describes "nice, cosy, little suppers," of which in his early youth he used to partake, at the house of his maternal grandfather, in Kentish Town. "He dined at two o'clock," observed the late proprietor of the *World*, "and had the most delightful suppers at nine; suppers of sprats, or kidneys, or tripe and onions; with foaming porter and hot grog afterwards."

I cannot share the enthusiasm possessed by some people for SPRATS, as an article of diet. When very "full-blown," the little fish make an excellent fertiliser for Marshal Niel roses; but as "winter whitebait," or sardines they are hardly up to "Derby form."

Sprats are not much encouraged at the fashionable hotels; and when tripe is brought to table, which is but rarely, that food is nearly always filleted, sprinkled with chopped parsley, and served with tomato sauce.

This is the sort of supper which is provided in the "gilt-edged" *caravanserais* of the metropolis, the following being a *verbatim* copy of a bill of fare at the Hotel Cecil:—

SOUPER, 5s.
Consommé Riche en tasses.
Laitances Frites, Villeroy.
Côte de Mouton aux Haricots Verts.
Chaudfroid de Mauviettes. Strasbourg evisie.
Salade.
Biscuit Cecil.

A lady-like repast this; and upon the whole, not dear. But roast loin of mutton hardly sounds tasty enough for a meal partaken of somewhere about the stroke of midnight. Still, such a supper is by no means calculated to "murder sleep." Upon the other hand it is a little difficult to credit the fact that the whole of the party invited by "My Lord Tomnoddy" to refresh themselves at the "Magpie and Stump," including the noble host himself, should have slumbered peacefully, with a noisy crowd in the street, after a supper which consisted of

SUPPER (*continued*)

**"To feed were best at home;
From thence the sauce to meat is ceremony;
Meeting were bare without it."**

Old supper-houses—The Early Closing Act—Evans's—Cremorne Gardens—The "Albion"—Parlour cookery—Kidneys fried in the fire-shovel—The true way to grill a bone—"Cannie Carle"—My lady's bower—Kidney dumplings—A Middleham supper—Steaks cut from a colt by brother to "Strafford" out of sister to "Bird on the Wing."

The Early Closing Act of 1872 had a disastrous effect upon the old London supper-houses. What Mr. John Hollingshead never tired of calling the "slap-me-and-put-me-to-bed law" rang the knell of many a licensed tavern, well-conducted, where plain, well-cooked food and sound liquor were to be obtained by men who would have astonished their respective couches had they sought them before the small hours.

Evans's.

The "Cave of Harmony" of Thackeray was a different place to the "Evans's" of my youthful days. Like the younger Newcome, I was taken there in the first instance, by the author of my being. But Captain Costigan was conspicuous by his absence; and "Sam Hall" was *non est*. I noted well the abnormal size of the broiled kidneys, and in my ignorance of anatomy, imagined that Evans's sheep must be subjected to somewhat the same process—the "ordeal by fire"—as the Strasbourg geese. And the potatoes—zounds, sirs! What potatoes! "Shall I turn it out, sir?" inquired the attentive waiter; and, as he seized the tuber, enveloped in the snow-white napkin, broke it in two, and ejected a floury pyramid upon my plate, I would, had I known of such a decoration in those days, have gladly recommended that attendant for the Distinguished Service order. In the course of many visits I never saw any supper commodity served here besides chops, steaks, kidneys, welsh-rarebits, poached eggs, and (I think) sausages; and the earliest impression made upon a youthful memory was the air of extreme confidence which pervaded the place. We certainly "remembered" the waiter; but not even a potato was paid for until we encountered the head functionary at the exit door; and his peculiar ideas of arithmetic would have given Bishop Colenso a succession of fits.

Who "Evans" was, we neither knew nor cared. "Paddy" Green, with his chronic smile, was enough for us; as he proffered his ever-ready snuff-box, inquired after our relatives—"Paddy," like "Spanky" at Eton, knew everybody—and implored silence whilst the quintette *Integer Vitæ* was being sung by the choir. We used to venerate that quintette far more than any music we ever heard in church, and I am certain "Paddy" Green would have backed his little pack of choristers—who, according to the general belief, passed the hours of daylight in waking the echoes of St. Paul's Cathedral, or Westminster Abbey, and therefore, at Evans's, always looked a bit stale and sleepy—against any choir in the world. As for Harry Sidney, the fat, jolly-looking gentleman who was wont to string together the topics of the day and reproduce them, fresh as rolls, set to music, we could never hear enough of him; and I wish I had now some of the half-crowns which in the past were bestowed upon Herr Von Joel, the indifferent *siffleur*, who was "permanently retained upon the premises," and who was always going to take a benefit the following week.

"Kidneys and 'armony"—that was the old programme in the "Cave." And then the march of time killed poor old Paddy, and another management reigned. Gradually the "lady element" was introduced, and a portion of the hall was set apart for the mixed assembly. And then came trouble, and, finally, disestablishment. And for some time before the closing of the Cave as a place of entertainment, it was customary to remove the fine old pictures (what became of them, I wonder), from the walls, at "Varsity Boat Race" time. For the undergraduate of those days was nothing if not rowdy. Youth will have its fling; and at Evans's the fling took the form of tumblers. Well do I recollect a fight in "the old style" in the very part of the "Cave" where eminent barristers, actors, and other wits of a past age, used to congregate. The premier boxer of Cambridge University had been exercising his undoubted talents as a breaker of glass, during the evening, and at length the overwrought manager obliged him with an opponent worthy of his fists in the person of a waiter who could also put up his fists. Several rounds were fought, strictly according to the rules of the Prize Ring, and in the result, whilst the waiter had sustained considerable damage to his ribs, the "Cambridge gent" had two very fine black eyes. Well do I remember that "mill," also the waiter, who afterwards became an habitual follower of the turf.

If Cremorne introduced the fashion of "long drinks," sodas, and et ceteras, the suppers served in the old gardens had not much to recommend them. A slice or two of cold beef, or a leg of a chicken, with some particularly salt ham, formed the average fare; but those who possessed their souls with patience occasionally saw something hot, in the way of food—chiefly cutlets. The great virtue of the cutlet is that it can be reheated; and one dish not infrequently did duty for more than one party. The rejected portion, in fact, would "reappear" as often as a retiring actor. "I know them salmon cutlets," the waiter in *Pink Dominoes* used to observe, "as well as I know my own mother!" In fact, Cremorne, like the "night houses" of old, was not an ideal place to sup at.

But, *per contra*, the "Albion" *was*. Until the enforcement of the "slap-me-and-put-me-to-bed" policy there was no more justly celebrated house of entertainment than the one which almost faced the stage door of Drury Lane theatre, in Great Russell Street. One of the brothers Cooper—another kept the Rainbow in Fleet Street—retired on a fortune made here, simply by pursuing the policy of giving his customers the best of everything. And a rare, Bohemian stamp of customers he had, too—a nice, large-hearted, open-handed lot of actors, successful and otherwise, dramatic critics ditto, and ditto journalists, also variegated in degree; with the usual, necessary, leavening of the "City" element. The custom of the fair sex was not encouraged at the old tavern; though in a room on the first floor they were permitted to sup, if in "the profession" and accompanied by males, whose manners and customs could be vouched for. In winter time, assorted grills, of fish, flesh, and fowl, were served as supper dishes; whilst tripe was the staple food. Welsh rarebits, too, were in immense demand. And I think it was here that I devoured, with no fear of the future before my plate, a

Buck Rarebit.

During the silent watches of the rest of the morning, bile and dyspepsia fought heroically for my soul; and yet the little animal is easy enough to prepare, being nothing grander than a Welsh rarebit, with a poached egg atop. But the little tins (silver, like the forks and spoons, until the greed and forgetfulness of mankind necessitated the substitution of electro-plate) which the Hebes at the "Old Cheshire Cheese" fill with fragments of the hostelry's godfather—subsequently to be stewed in good old ale—are less harmful to the interior of the human diaphragm.

A favourite Albion supper-dish during the summer months was

Lamb's Head and Mince.

I have preserved the recipe, a gift from one of the waiters—but whether Ponsford, Taylor, or "Shakespeare" (so-called because he bore not the faintest resemblance to the immortal bard) I forget—and here it is:

> The head should be scalded, scraped, and well washed. Don't have it singed, in the Scottish fashion, as lamb's wool is not nice to eat. Then put it, with the liver (the sweetbread was chopped up with the brain, I fancy), into a stewpan, with a Spanish onion stuck with cloves, a bunch of parsley, a little thyme, a carrot, a turnip, a bay leaf, some crushed peppercorns, a tablespoonful of salt, and half a gallon of cold water. Let it boil up, skim, and then simmer for an hour. Divide the head, take out the tongue and brain, and dry the rest of the head in a cloth. Mince the liver and tongue, season with salt and pepper, and simmer in the original gravy (thickened) for half-an-hour. Brush the two head-halves with yolk of egg, grate bread crumbs over, and bake in oven. The brain and sweetbread to be chopped and made into cakes, fried, and then placed in the dish around the head-halves.

Ah me! The old tavern, after falling into bad ways, entertaining "extra-ladies" and ruined gamesters, has been closed for years. The ground floor was a potato warehouse the last time I passed the place. And it should be mentioned that the actors, journalists, etc., who, in the 'seventies, possessed smaller means, or more modest ambitions, were in the habit of supping—on supping days—at a cheaper haunt in the Strand, off (alleged) roast goose. But, according to one Joseph Eldred, a comedian of some note and shirt-cuff, the meat which was apportioned to us here was, in reality, always bullock's heart, sliced, and with a liberal allowance of sage and onions. "It's the seasoning as does it," observed Mr. Samuel Weller.

Then there was another Bohemian house of call, and supper place, in those nights—the "Occidental," once known as the "Coal Hole," where, around a large, beautifully polished mahogany table, many of the wits of the town —"Harry" Leigh and "Tom" Purnell were two of the inveterates—sat, and devoured Welsh rarebits, and other things. The house, too, could accommodate not a few lodgers; and one of its great charms was that nobody cared a button what time you retired to your couch, or what time you ordered breakfast. In these matters, the Occidental resembled the "Limmer's" of the "Billy Duff" era, and the "Lane's" of my own dear subaltern days.

Parlour Cookery.

It was after the last-named days that, whilst on tour with various dramatic combinations—more from necessity than art, as far as I was concerned—that the first principles of parlour cookery became impregnated in mine understanding. We were not all "stars," although we did our best. Salaries were (according to the advertisements) "low but sure"; and (according to experiences) by no means as sure as death, or taxes. The "spectre" did not invariably assume his "martial stalk," of a Saturday; and cheap provincial lodgings do not hold out any extra inducement in the way of cookery. So, whilst we endured the efforts of the good landlady at the early dinner, some of us determined to dish up our own suppers. For the true artist never really feels (or never used to feel, at all events) like "picking a bit" until merely commercial folks have gone to bed.

Many a time and oft, with the aid of a cigar box (empty, of course), a couple of books, and an arrangement of plates, have I prepared a savoury supper of mushrooms, toasted cheese, or a *kebob* of larks, or other small fowl, in front of the fire. More than once have I received notice to quit the next morning for grilling kidneys on the perforated portion of a handsome and costly steel fire-shovel. And by the time I had become sufficiently advanced in culinary science to stew tripe and onions, in an enamel-lined saucepan, the property of the "responsible gent," we began to give ourselves airs. Landladies' ideas on the subject of supper for "theatricals," it may be mentioned, seldom soared above yeast dumplings. And few of us liked the name, even, of yeast dumplings.

But perhaps the champion effort of all was when I was sojourning in the good city of Carlisle—known to its inhabitants by the pet name of "Cannie Carle." A good lady was, for her sins, providing us with board and lodging, in return for (promised) cash. My then companion was a merry youth who afterwards achieved fame by writing the very funniest and one of the most successful of three-act farces that was ever placed upon the stage. Now there is not much the matter with a good joint of ribs of beef, roasted to a turn. But when that beef is placed on the table hot for the Sunday dinner, and cold at every succeeding meal until finished up, one's appetite for the flesh of the ox begins to slacken. So we determined on the Wednesday night to "strike" for a tripe supper.

"Indeed," protested the good landlady, "ye'll get nae tripe in this hoose, cannie men. Hae ye no' got guid beef, the noo?"

Late that night we had grilled bones for supper; not the ordinary

Grilled Bones

which you get in an eating house, but a vastly superior article. We, or rather my messmate, cut a rib from off the aforementioned beef, scored the flesh across, and placed the bone in the centre of a beautifully clear fire which had been specially prepared. It was placed there by means of the tongs—a weapon of inestimable value in Parlour Cookery—and withdrawn by the same medium. Some of the black wanted scraping off the surface of the meat, but the grill was a perfect dream. The GUBBINS SAUCE, already mentioned in this volume, had not at that time been invented; but as I was never without a bottle of TAPP SAUCE—invaluable for Parlour Cookery; you can get it at Stembridge's—we had plenty of relish. Then we severed another rib from the carcase, and served it in the same manner. For it was winter time and we had wearied of frigid ox.

Next morning the landlady's face was a study. I rather think that after some conversation, we propitiated her with an order for two for the dress circle; but it is certain that we had tripe that evening.

An ideal supper in *miladi's boudoir* is associated, in the writer's mind, with rose-coloured draperies, dainty china, a cosy fire, a liberal display of *lingerie,* a strong perfume of heliotrope and orris root—and *miladi* herself. When next she invites her friends, she will kindly order the following repast to be spread:—

Clear soup, in cups.
Fillets of soles Parisienne.
Chaudfroid of Quails.
Barded sweetbreads.
Perigord pâté.

By way of contrast, let me quote a typical supper-dish which the "poor player" used to order, when he could afford it.

Kidney Dumpling.

Cut a large Spanish onion in half. Take out the heart, and substitute a sheep's kidney, cut into four. Season with salt and pepper, join the two halves, and enclose in a paste. Bake on a buttered tin, in a moderate oven, for about an hour.

N.B.—Be sure the cook *bakes* this dumpling, as it is not nice boiled.

An artistic friend who at one time of his life resided near the great horse-training centre of Middleham, in Yorkshire, gave a steak supper at the principal inn, to some of the stable attendants. The fare was highly approved of.

"Best Scotch beef I ever put tooth into!" observed the "head lad" at old Tom Lawson's stables.

"Ah!" returned the host, who was a bit of a wag, "your beef was cut from a colt of Lord Glasgow's that was thought highly of at one time; and he was shot the day before yesterday."

"Thou didst eat strange flesh,
Which some did die to look on."

> The ups and downs of life—Stirring adventures—Marching on to glory—Shooting in the tropics—Pepper-pot—With the *Rajah Sahib*—Goat-sacrifices at breakfast time—Simla to Cashmere—Manners and customs of Thibet—Burmah—No place to get fat in—Insects—Voracity of the natives—Snakes—Sport in the Jungle—Loaded for snipe, sure to meet tiger—With the gippos—No baked hedgehog—Cheap milk.

The intelligent reader may have gathered from some of the foregoing pages that the experiences of the writer have been of a variegated nature. As an habitual follower of the Turf once observed:

> "When we're rich we rides in chaises,
> And when we're broke we walks like ——"

Never mind what. It was an evil man who said it, but he was a philosopher. Dinner in the gilded saloon one day, on the next no dinner at all, and the key of the street. Such is life!

Those experiences do not embrace a mortal combat with a "grizzly" in the Rockies, nor a tramp through a miasma-laden forest in Darkest Africa, with nothing better to eat than poisonous *fungi*, assorted grasses, red ants, and dwarfs; nor yet a bull fight. But they include roughing it in the bush, on underdone bread and scorched kangaroo, a tramp from Benares to the frontier of British India, another tramp or two some way beyond that frontier, a dreadful journey across the eternal snows of the Himalayas, a day's shooting in the Khyber Pass, a railway accident in Middlesex, a mad elephant (he had killed seven men, one of them blind) hunt at Thayet Myoo, in British Burmah, a fine snake anecdote or two, a night at Cambridge with an escaped lunatic, a tiger story (of course), and a capture for debt by an officer of the Sheriff of Pegu, with no other clothing on his body than a short jacket of gaily coloured silk, and a loin cloth. My life's history is never likely to be written—chiefly through sheer laziness on my own part, and the absence of the gambling instinct on that of the average publisher—but like the brown gentleman who smothered his wife, I have "seen things."

In this chapter no allusion will be made to "up river" delights, the only idea of "camping out" which is properly understood by the majority of "up to date" young men and maidens; for this theme has been already treated, most comically and delightfully, by Mr. Jerome, in the funniest book I ever read. My own camping experiences have been for the most part in foreign lands, though I have seen the sun rise, whilst reclining beneath the Royal trees in St. James's Park; and as this book is supposed to deal with gastronomy, rather than adventure, a brief sketch of camp life must suffice.

On the march! What a time those who "served the Widdy"—by which disrespectful term, our revered Sovereign was *not* known in those days—used to have before the continent of India had been intersected by the railroad! The absence of one's proper *quantum* of rest, the forced marches over *kutcha* (imperfectly made) bye-roads, the sudden changes of temperature, raids of the native thief, the troubles with "bobbery" camels, the still more exasperating behaviour of the *bail-wallahs* (bullock-drivers), the awful responsibilities of the officer-on-baggage-guard, on active duty, often in the saddle for fifteen hours at a stretch, the absolutely necessary cattle-raids, by the roadside—all these things are well known to those who have undergone them, but are far too long "another story" to be related here. As for the food partaken of during a march with the regiment, the bill-of-fare differed but little from that of the cantonments; but the officer who spent a brief holiday in a shooting expedition had to "rough it" in more ways than one.

There was plenty of game all over the continent in my youthful days, and the average shot need not have lacked a dinner, even if he had not brought with him a consignment of "Europe" provisions. English bread was lacking, certainly, and biscuits, native or otherwise—"otherwise" for choice, as the bazaar article tasted principally of pin-cushions and the smoke of dried and lighted cow-dung—or the ordinary *chupatti*, the flat, unleavened cake, which the poor Indian manufactures for his own consumption. Cold tea is by far the best liquid to carry—or rather to have carried for you—whilst actually shooting; but the weary sportsman will require something more exciting, and more poetical, on his return to camp. As for solid fare it was usually

Pepper-pot

for dinner, day by day. We called it Pepper-pot—that is to say, although it differed somewhat from the West Indian concoction of that name, for which the following is the recipe:—

> Put the remains of any cold flesh or fowl into a saucepan, and cover with *cassaripe*—which has been already described in the Curry chapter as extract of Manioc root. Heat up the stew and serve.

Our pepper-pot was usually made in a gipsy-kettle, suspended from a tripod. The foundation of the stew was always a tin of some kind of soup. Then a few goat chops—mutton is bad to buy out in the jungle—and then any bird or beast that may have been shot, divided into fragments. I have frequently made a stew of this sort, with so many ingredients in it that the flavour when served out at table—or on the bullock-trunk which often did duty for a table—would have beaten the wit of man to describe. There was hare soup "intil't" (as the Scotsman said to the late Prince Consort), and a collop or two of buffalo-beef, with snipe, quails, and jungle-fowl. There were half the neck of an antelope and a few sliced onions lurking within the bowl. And there were potatoes "intil't," and plenty of pepper and salt. And for lack of cassaripe we flavoured the savoury mess with mango chutnee and Tapp sauce. And if any cook, English or foreign, can concoct a more worthy dish than this, or more grateful to the palate, said cook can come my way.

The old *dak gharry* method of travelling in India may well come under the head of Camping Out. In the hot weather we usually progressed—or got emptied into a ditch—or collided with something else, during the comparative "coolth" of the night; resting (which in Hindustan usually means perspiring and calling the country names) all day at one or other of the *dak bungalows* provided by a benevolent Government for the use of the wandering *sahib*. The larder at one of those rest-houses was seldom well filled. Although the *khansamah* who prostrated himself in the sand at your approach would declare that he was prepared to supply everything which the protector-of-the-poor might deign to order, it would be found on further inquiry that the *khansamah* had, like the Player Queen in Hamlet, protested too much—that he was a natural romancer. And his "everything" usually resolved itself into a "spatch-cock," manufactured from the spectral rooster, who had heralded the approach of the *sahib's* caravan.

A Rajah's

ideas of hospitality are massive. Labouring under the belief that the white *sahib* when not eating must necessarily be drinking, the commissariat arrangements of Rajahdom are on a colossal scale—for the chief benefit of his *major domo*. I might have bathed in dry champagne, had the idea been pleasing, whilst staying with a certain genial prince, known to irreverent British subalterns as "Old Coppertail"; whilst the bedroom furniture was on the same liberal scale. True, I lay on an ordinary native *charpoy*, which might have been bought in the bazaar for a few *annas*, but there was a grand piano in one corner of the apartment, and a buhl cabinet containing rare china in another. There was a coloured print of the Governor-General over the doorway, and an oil painting of the Judgment of Solomon over the mantelshelf. And on a table within easy reach of the bed was a silver-plated dinner service, decked with fruits and sweetmeats, and tins of salmon, and pots of Guava jelly and mixed pickles, and two tumblers, each of which would have easily held a week-old baby. And there was a case of champagne beneath that table, with every appliance for cutting wires and extracting the corks.

Another time the writer formed one of a small party invited to share the hospitality of a potentate, whose estate lay on the snowy side of Simla. The fleecy element, however, was not in evidence in June, the month of our visit, although towards December Simla herself is usually wrapt in the white mantle, and garrisoned by monkeys, who have fled from the land of ice. Tents had been erected for us in a barren-looking valley, somewhat famous, however, for the cultivation of potatoes. There was an annual celebration of some sort, the day after our arrival, and for breakfast that morning an *al fresco* meal had been prepared for us, almost within whispering distance of an heathen temple. And it *was* a breakfast! There was a turkey stuffed with a fowl, to make the breast larger, and there was a "Europe" ham. A tin of lobster, a bottle of pickled walnuts, a dreadful concoction, alleged to be an omelette, but looking more like the sole of a tennis shoe, potatoes, boiled eggs, a dish of Irish stew, a fry of small fish, a weird-looking curry, a young goat roasted whole, and a plum pudding!

The tea had hardly been poured out—Kussowlie beer, Epps's cocoa, and (of course) champagne, and John Exshaw's brandy were also on tap—when a gentleman with very little on proceeded to decapitate a goat at the foot of the temple steps. This was somewhat startling, but when the (presumed) high-priest chopped off the head of another bleating victim, our meal was interrupted. The executions had been carried out in very simple fashion. First, the priest sprinkled a little water on the neck of the victim (who was held in position by an assistant), and then retired up the steps. Then, brandishing a small sickle, he rushed back, and in an instant off went the head, which was promptly carried, reeking with gore, within the temple. But if, as happened more than once, the head was not sliced off at the initial attempt, it was left on the ground when decapitation had been at length effected. The deity inside was evidently a bit particular!

Nine goats had been sacrificed, ere our remonstrances were attended to; and we were allowed to pursue our meal in peace. But I don't think anybody had goat for breakfast that morning.

Later on, the fun of the fair commenced, and the *paharis*, or hill men, trooped in from miles round, with their sisters, cousins, and aunts. Their wives, we imagined, were too busily occupied in carrying their accustomed loads of timber to and fro. Your Himalayan delights in a fair, and the numerous swings and roundabouts were all well patronised; whilst the jugglers, and the snake charmers—in many instances it was difficult to tell at a glance which was charmer and which snake—were all well patronised. Later on, when the lamps had been lit, a *burra nâtch* was started, and the Bengali Baboos who had come all the way from Simla in *dhoolies* to be present at this, applauded vigorously. And our host being in constant dread lest we should starve to death or expire of thirst, never tired of bidding us to a succession of banquets at which we simply went through the forms of eating, to please him. And just when we began to get sleepy these simple hill folks commenced to dance amongst themselves. They were just a little monotonous, their choregraphic efforts. Parties of men linked arms and sidled around fires of logs, singing songs of their mountain homes the while. And as they were evidently determined to make a night of it, sleep for those who understood not the game, with their tents close handy, was out of the question. And when, as soon as we could take our departure decently and decorously, we started up the hill again, those doleful monotonous dances were still in progress, although the fires were out, and the voices decidedly husky. A native of the Himalayas is nothing if not energetic—in his own interests be it understood.

A few months later I formed one of a small party who embarked on a more important expedition than the last named, although we traversed the same road. It is a journey which has frequently been made since, from Simla to Cashmere, going as far into the land of the Great Llama as the inhabitants will allow the stranger to do—which is not very far; but, in the early sixties there were but few white men who had even skirted Thibet. In the afternoon of life, when stirring the fire has become preferable to stirring adventure, it seems (to the writer at all events) very like an attempt at self-slaughter to have travelled so many hundreds of miles along narrow goatpaths, with a *khud* (precipice) of thousands of feet on one side or the other; picking one's way, if on foot, over the frequent avalanche (or "land slip," as we called it in those days) of shale or granite; or if carried in a *dhoolie*—which is simply a hammock attached by straps to a bamboo pole—running the risk of being propelled over a precipice by your heathen carriers. It is not the pleasantest of sensations to cross a mountain torrent by means of a frail bridge (called a *jhula*) of ropes made from twigs, and stretched many feet above the torrent itself, nor to "weather" a corner, whilst clinging tooth and nail to the face of a cliff. And when there is any riding to be done, most people would prefer a hill pony to a *yak*, the native ox of Thibet. By far the best part of a *yak* is his beautiful silky, fleecy tail, which is largely used in Hindustan, by dependants of governors-general, commanders-in-chief, and other mighty ones, for the discomfiture of the frequent fly. A very little equestrian exercise on the back of a *yak* goes a long way; and if given my choice, I would sooner ride a stumbling cab-horse in a saddle with spikes in it.

But those days were our salad ones; we were not only "green of judgment," but admirers of the beautiful, and reckless of danger. But it was decidedly "roughing it." As it is advisable to traverse that track as lightly laden as possible, we took but few "Europe" provisions with us, depending upon the villages, for the most part, for our supplies. We usually managed to buy a little flour, wherewith to make the inevitable *chupati*, and at some of the co-operative stores *en route,* we obtained mutton of fair flavour. We did not know in those days that flesh exposed to the air, in the higher ranges of the Himalayas, will not putrefy, else we should have doubtless made a species of *biltong* of the surplus meat, to carry with us in case of any famine about. So "short commons" frequently formed the bill of fare. Our little stock of brandy was carefully husbanded, against illness; and, judging from the subsequent histories of two of the party, this was the most miraculous feature of the expedition. For liquid refreshment we had neat water, and *thé à la mode de Thibet*. Doctor Nansen, in his book on the crossing of Greenland, inveighs strongly against the use of alcohol in an Arctic expedition; but I confess that the first time I tasted Thibet tea I would have given both my ears for a soda and brandy. The raw tea was compressed into the shape of a brick, with the aid of—we did not inquire what; its infusion was drunk, either cold or lukewarm, flavoured with salt, and a small lump of butter which in any civilised police court would have gained the vendor a month's imprisonment without the option of a fine.

The people of the district were in the habit of gorging themselves with flesh when they could get it; and polyandry was another of their pleasant customs. We saw one lady who was married to three brothers, but did not boast of it. Thibet is probably the most priest-ridden country in the world, and ought to be the most religious; for the natives can grind out their prayers, on wheels, at short intervals, in pretty much the same way as we grind our coffee in dear old England.

But we reached the promised land at last; and here at least there was no lack of food and drink. Meat was cheap in those days; and one of the party, without any bargaining whatever, purchased a sheep for eight annas, or one shilling sterling. Mutton is not quite as cheap at the time of writing this book (1897), I believe; but in the long ago there were but few English visitors to the land of Lalla Rookh, and those who did go had to obtain permission of the Rajah, through the British Resident.

With improved transit, and a railroad from Rangoon to Mandalay, matters gastronomic may be better in British Burmah nowadays; but in the course of an almost world-wide experience I have never enjoyed food less than in Pagoda-land during the sixties. And as a Burmese built house was not a whit more comfortable than a tent, and far less waterproof, this subject may well be included in the chapter headed "Camping Out." Fruits there were, varied and plentiful; and if you only planted the crown of a pine-apple in your compound one evening you would probably find a decent-sized pine-apple above ground next—well, next week. At least so they told me when I arrived in the country. This fruit, in fact, was so plentiful that we used to peel the pines, and gnaw them, just like a school-boy would gnaw the ordinary variety of apple. But we had no mutton—not up the country, that is to say; and we were entirely dependent upon Madras for potatoes. Therefore, as there was only a steamer once a month from Madras to Rangoon, which invariably missed the Irrawaddy monthly mail-boat, we "exiles" had to content ourselves with yams, or the abominable "preserved" earth-apple. The insects of the air wrestled with us at the mess-table, for food; and the man who did not swallow an evil-tasting fly of some sort in his soup was lucky.[9] As for the food of the Burman himself, "absolutely beastly" was no name for it. Strips of cat-fish the colour of beef were served at his marriage feasts; and he was especially fond of a condiment the name of which was pronounced *nuppee*—although that is probably not the correct spelling, and I never studied the language of that country—which was concocted from a smaller description of fish, buried in the earth until decomposition had triumphed, and then mashed up with *ghee* (clarified—and "postponed"—butter). There was, certainly, plenty of shooting to be obtained in the district; but, as it rained in torrents for nine months in every year, the shooter required a considerable amount of nerve, and, in addition to a Boyton suit, case-hardened lungs and throat. And, singularly enough, it was an established fact that if loaded for snipe you invariably met a tiger, or something else with sharp teeth, and *vice versa*. Also, you were exceptionally fortunate if you did not step upon one of the venomous snakes of the country, of whom the *hamadryad's* bite was said to be fatal within five minutes. I had omitted to mention that snake is also a favourite food of the Burman; and as I seldom went home of an evening without finding a rat-snake or two in the verandah, or the arm-chair, the natives had snake for breakfast, most days. The rat-snake is, however, quite harmless to life.

I have "camped out" in England once or twice; once with a select circle of gipsies, the night before the Derby. I wished merely to study character; and, after giving them a few words of the Romany dialect, and a good deal of tobacco, I was admitted into their confidences. But the experience gained was not altogether pleasing, nor yet edifying; nor did we have baked hedgehog for supper. In fact I have never yet met the "gippo" (most of them keep fowls) who will own to having tasted this *bonne bouche* of the descriptive writer. Possibly this is on account of the scarcity of the hedgehog. "Tea-kettle broth"—bread sopped in water, with a little salt and dripping to flavour the soup—on the other hand, figures on most of the gipsy *menus*. And upon one occasion, very early in the morning, another wanderer and the writer obtained much-needed liquid refreshment by milking the yield of a Jersey cow into each other's mouths, alternately. But this was a long time ago, and in the neighbourhood of Bagshot Heath, and it was somebody else's cow; so let no more be said about it.

I fear this chapter is not calculated to make many mouths water. In fact what in the world has brought it into the midst of a work on gastronomy I am at a loss to make out. However here it is.

COMPOUND DRINKS

**"Flow wine! Smile woman!
And the universe is consoled."**

Derivation of punch—"Five"—The "milk" brand—The best materials—Various other punches—Bischoff or Bishop—"Halo" punch—Toddy—The toddy tree of India—Flip—A "peg"—John Collins—Out of the guard-room.

The subject of PUNCH is such an important one that it may be placed first on the list of dainty beverages which can be made by the art or application of man or woman.

First, let us take the origin of the word. DOCTOR KITCHENER, an acknowledged authority, during his lifetime, on all matters connected with eating and drinking, has laid it down that punch is of West Indian origin, and that the word when translated, means "five"; because there be five ingredients necessary in the concoction of the beverage. But Doctor Kitchener and his disciples (of whom there be many) may go to the bottom of the cookery class; for although from the large connection which rum and limes have with the mixture, there would seem to be a West Indian flavour about it; the word "five," when translated into West Indianese, is nothing like "punch." Having satisfied themselves that this is a fact, modern authorities have tried the East Indies for the source of the name, and have discovered that *panch* in Hindustani really does mean "five." "Therefore," says one modern authority, "it is named punch from the five ingredients which compose it—(1) spirit, (2) acid, (3) spice, (4) sugar, (5) water." Another modern authority calls punch "a beverage introduced into England from India, and so called from being usually made of five (Hindi, *panch*) ingredients—arrack, tea, sugar, water, and lemon juice." This sounds far more like an East Indian concoction than the other; but at the same time punch—during the latter half of the nineteenth century at all events—was as rare a drink in Hindustan as *bhang* in Great Britain. The *panch* theory is an ingenious one, but there are plenty of other combinations (both liquid and solid) of five to which the word punch is never applied; and about the last beverage recommended by the faculty for the consumption of the sojourner in the land of the Great Mogul, would, I should think, be the entrancing, seductive one which we Britons know under the name of punch. Moreover it is not every punch-concoctor who uses five ingredients. In the minds of some—youthful members of the Stock Exchange, for the most part—water is an altogether unnecessary addition to the alcoholic mixture which is known by the above name. And what manner of man would add spice to that delight of old Ireland, "a jug o' punch?" On the other hand, in many recipes, there are more than five ingredients used.

But after all, the origin of the name is of but secondary importance, as long as you can make punch. Therefore, we will commence with a few recipes for

Milk Punch.

1. Three bottles of rum.
The most delicately-flavoured rum is the "Liquid Sunshine" brand.
One bottle of sherry.
13 lbs of loaf-sugar.
The rind of six lemons, and the juice of twelve.
One quart of boiling skimmed milk.

Mix together, let the mixture stand eight days, stirring it each day. Strain and bottle, and let it stand three months. Then re-bottle, and let the bottles lie on their sides in the cellar for two years, to mature. The flavour will be much better than if drunk after the first period of three months.

It is not everybody, however, who would care to wait two years, three months, and eight days for the result of his efforts in punch-making. Therefore another recipe may be appended; and in this one no "close time" is laid down for the consumption of the mixture.

2. Put into a bottle of rum or brandy the thinly-pared rinds of three Seville oranges, and three lemons. Cork tightly for two days. Rub off on 2 lbs of lump sugar the rinds of six lemons, squeeze the juice from the whole of the fruit over the 2 lbs of sugar, add three quarts of boiling water, one of boiling milk, half a teaspoonful of nutmeg, and mix all thoroughly well together until the sugar is dissolved. Pour in the rum or brandy, stir, and strain till clear; bottle closely.

There is more than one objection to this recipe. (1) Rum, and not brandy (by itself), should be used for milk punch. (2) There is an "intolerable amount" of water; and (3) the nutmeg had better remain in the spice-box.

3. Cut off the thin yellow rind of four lemons and a Seville orange, taking care not to include even a fragment of the *white* rind, and place in a basin. Pour in one pint of Jamaica rum, and let it stand, covered over, twelve hours. Then strain, and mix with it one pint of lemon juice, and two pints of cold water, in which one pound of sugar-candy has been dissolved; add the whites of two eggs, beaten to a froth, three pints more of rum, one pint of madeira, one pint of strong green tea, and a large wine-glassful of maraschino. Mix thoroughly, and pour over all one pint of boiling milk. Let the punch stand a little while, then strain through a jelly-bag, and either use at once, or bottle off.

Here let it be added, lest the precept be forgotten, that the

Very best Materials

are absolutely necessary for the manufacture of punch, as of other compound drinks. In the above recipe for instance by "madeira," is meant "Rare Old East Indian," and *not* marsala, which wine, in French kitchens, is invariably used as the equivalent of madeira. There must be no inferior sherry, Gladstone claret, cheap champagne, nor potato-brandy, used for any of my recipes, or I will not be responsible for the flavour of the beverage. The following is the best idea of a milk punch known to the writer:—

4. Over the yellow rind of four lemons and one Seville orange, pour one pint of rum. Let it stand, covered over, for twelve hours. Strain and

mix in two pints more of rum, one pint of brandy, one pint of sherry, half-a-pint of lemon juice, the expressed juice of a peeled pine-apple, one pint of green tea, one pound of sugar dissolved in one quart of boiling water, the whites of two eggs beaten up, one quart of boiling milk. Mix well, let it cool, and then strain through a jelly-bag, and bottle off.

This punch is calculated to make the epicure forget that he has just been partaking of conger-eel broth instead of clear turtle.

Cambridge Milk Punch.

This a fairly good boys' beverage, there being absolutely "no offence in't." Put the rind of half a lemon (small) into one pint of new milk, with twelve lumps of sugar. Boil very slowly for fifteen minutes, then remove from the fire, take out the lemon rind, and mix in the yolk of one egg, which has been previously blended with one tablespoonful of cold milk, two tablespoonfuls of brandy, and four of rum. Whisk all together, and when the mixture is frothed, it is ready to serve.

Oxford Punch.

There is no milk in this mixture, which sounds like "for'ard on!" for the undergraduate who for the first time samples it.

Rub off the yellow rind of three lemons with half-a-pound of loaf sugar. Put the result into a large jug, with the yellow rind of one Seville orange, the juice of three Seville oranges and eight lemons, and one pint of liquefied calf's-foot jelly. Mix thoroughly, then pour over two quarts of boiling water, and set the jug on the hob for thirty minutes. Strain the mixture into a punch-bowl, and when cool add one small bottle of capillaire (an infusion of maidenhair fern, flavoured with sugar and orange-flower water); one pint of brandy, one pint of rum, half-a-pint of dry sherry, and one quart of orange shrub—a mixture of orange-peel, juice, sugar, and rum.

After drinking this, the young student will be in a fit state to sally forth, with his fellows, and "draw" a Dean, or drown an amateur journalist.

I have a very old recipe, in MS., for "Bischoff," which I take to be the original of the better known beverage called "Bishop," for the manufacture of which I have also directions. For the sake of comparison I give the two.

Bischoff.

Cut into four parts each, three Seville oranges, and slightly score the rinds across with a sharp knife. Roast the quarters lightly before a slow fire, and put them into a bowl with two bottles of claret, with a little cinnamon and nutmeg. Infuse this mixture over a slow heat for five or six hours, then pass it through a jelly-bag, and sweeten. It may be drunk hot or cold, but in any case must never be allowed to boil.

Bishop.

Two drachmas each of cloves, mace, ginger, cinnamon, and allspice, boiled in half-a-pint of water for thirty minutes. Strain. Put a bottle of port in a saucepan over the fire, add the spiced infusion, and a lemon stuck with six cloves. Whilst this is heating gradually—it must not boil—take four ounces of loaf sugar, and with the lumps grate off the outer rind of a lemon into a punch-bowl. Add the sugar, and juice, and the hot wine, etc. Add another bottle of port, and serve either hot or cold.

I am prepared to lay a shade of odds on the "op" against the "off."

Another old recipe has been quoted in some of my earlier public efforts, under different names. I have improved considerably upon the proportion of the ingredients, and now hand the whole back, under the name of

Halo Punch.

With a quarter pound of loaf sugar rub off the outer rind of one lemon and two Seville oranges. Put rind and sugar into a large punch-bowl with the juice and pulp, mix the sugar well with the juice and one teacupful of boiling water, and stir till cold. Add half-a-pint of pine-apple syrup, one pint of strong green tea, a claret-glassful of maraschino, a smaller glassful of noyeau, half-a-pint of white rum, one pint of brandy, and one bottle of champagne. Strain and serve, having, if necessary, added more sugar.

Note well the proportions. This is the same beverage which some Cleveland friends of mine, having read the recipe, thought *boiling* would improve. The result was—well, a considerable amount of chaos.

Glasgow Punch.

The following is from *Peter's Letters to his Kinsfolk,* and is from the pen of John Gibson Lockhart:—

> The sugar being melted with a little *cold* water, the artist squeezed about a dozen lemons through a wooden strainer, and then poured in water enough almost to fill the bowl. In this state the liquor goes by the name of sherbet, and a few of the connoisseurs in his immediate neighbourhood were requested to give their opinion of it—for in the mixing of the sherbet lies, according to the Glasgow creed, at least one-half of the whole battle. This being approved of by an audible smack from the lips of the umpires, the rum was added to the beverage, I suppose, in something about the proportion from one to seven.

Does this mean one of sherbet and seven of rum, or the converse?

> Last of all, the maker cut a few limes, and running each section rapidly round the rim of his bowl, squeezed in enough of this more delicate acid to flavour the whole composition. In this consists the true *tour-de-maitre* of the punch-maker.

Well, possibly; but it seems a plainish sort of punch; and unless the rum be allowed to preponderate, most of us would be inclined to call the mixture lemonade. And I do not believe that since Glasgow has been a city its citizens ever drank much of *that*.

A few more punches, and then an anecdote.

Ale Punch.

One quart of mild ale in a bowl, add one wine-glassful of brown sherry, the same quantity of old brandy, a tablespoonful of sifted sugar, the peel and juice of one lemon, a grate of nutmeg, and an iceberg.

N.B.—Do not insert old ale, by mistake. And for my own part, I think it a mistake to mix John Barleycorn with wine (except champagne) and spirits.

Barbadoes Punch.

A tablespoonful of raspberry syrup, a ditto of sifted sugar, a wine-glassful of water, double that quantity of brandy, half a wine-glassful of guava jelly, liquid, the juice of half a lemon, two slices of orange, one slice of pine-apple, in a long tumbler. Ice and shake well and drink through straws.

Curaçoa Punch.

Put into a large tumbler one tablespoonful of sifted sugar, one wine-glassful of brandy, the same quantity of water, half a wine-glassful of Jamaica rum, a wine-glassful of curaçoa, and the juice of half a lemon; fill the tumbler with crushed ice, shake, and drink through straws.

Grassot Punch.

This has nothing to do with warm asparagus, so have no fear. It is simply another big-tumbler mixture, of one wine-glassful of brandy, a liqueur-glassful of curaçoa, a squeeze of lemon, two teaspoonfuls sugar, one of syrup of strawberries, one wine-glassful of water, and the thin rind of a lemon; fill up the tumbler with crushed ice, shake, and put slices of ripe apricots atop. Drink how you like.

Most of the above are hot-weather beverages, and the great beauty of some of them will be found in the small quantity of water in the mixture. Here is a punch which may be drunk in any weather, and either hot or cold.

Regent Punch.

Pour into a bowl a wine-glassful of champagne, the same quantities of hock, curaçoa, rum, and madeira. Mix well, and add a pint of boiling tea, sweetened. Stir well and serve.

Apropos of the derivation of "punch," I was unaware until quite recently that Messrs. Bradbury's & Agnew's little paper had any connection therewith. But I was assured by one who knew all about it, that such was the case.

"What?" I exclaimed. "How can the *London Charivari* possibly have anything to do with this most seductive of beverages?"

"My dear fellow," was the reply, "have you never heard of Mark *Lemon*?"

I turned to smite him hip and thigh; but the jester had fled.

And now a word or two as to "Toddy." One of the authorities quoted in the punch difficulty declares that toddy is also an Indian drink. So it is. But that drink no more resembles what is known in more civilised lands as toddy than I resemble the late king Solomon. The palm-sap which the poor Indian distils into arrack and occasionally drinks in its natural state for breakfast after risking his neck in climbing trees to get it, can surely have no connection with hot whisky and water? Yet the authority says so; but he had best be careful ere he promulgates his theory in the presence of Scotsmen and others who possess special toddy-glasses. This is how I make

Whisky Toddy.

The Irish call this whisky punch. But do not let us wrangle over the name. Into an ordinary-sized tumbler which has been warmed, put one average lump of sugar, a ring of thin lemon peel, and a silver teaspoon. Fill the tumbler one quarter full of water as near boiling point as possible. Cover over until the sugar be dissolved and peel be infused.

Then add one wine-glassful—not a small one—of the best whisky you can find—the "Pollok" brand, and the "R.B." are both excellent. Then drink the toddy, or punch; for should you attempt to add any more water you will incur the lifelong contempt of every Irishman or Scotsman who may be in the same room. If Irish whisky be used, of course you will select "John Jameson."

'Twixt ale-flip and egg-flip there is not much more difference than 'twixt tweedledum and tweedledee. Both are equally "more-ish" on a cold evening; and no Christmas eve is complete without a jug of one or the other.

Ale-flip.

Pour into a saucepan three pints of mild ale, one tablespoonful of sifted sugar, a blade of mace, a clove, and a small piece of butter; and bring the liquor to a boil. Beat up in a basin the white of one egg and the yolks of two, mixed with about a wine-glassful of cold ale. Mix all together in the saucepan, then pour into a jug, and thence into another jug, from a height, for some minutes, to froth the flip thoroughly but do not let it get cold.

Egg-flip.

Heat one pint of ale, and pour into a jug. Add two eggs, beaten with three ounces of sugar, and pour the mixture from one jug to the other, as in the preceding recipe. Grate a little nutmeg and ginger over the flip before serving.

Were I to ask What is

A Peg?

I should probably be told that a peg was something to hang something or somebody else on, or that it was something to be driven through or into something else. And the latter would be the more correct answer, for at the time of my sojourn in the great continent of India, a peg meant a large brandy-and-soda. At that time whisky was but little known in Punkahland, and was only used high up in the Punjaub during the "cold weather"—and it is cold occasionally in that region, where for some months they are enabled to make ice—but that is *une autre histoire*. Rum I once tasted at Simla, and gin will be dealt with presently. But since the visit of H.R.H. the Prince of Wales, a peg has always signified a *whisky*-and-soda. And yet we have not heard of any particular decrease in the death-rate. Despite what those who have only stayed a month or two in the country have committed to print, alcohol is *not* more fatal in a tropical country than a temperate one. But you must not overdo your alcohol. I have seen a gay young spark, a fine soldier, and over six feet in height, drink *eight* pegs of a morning, ere he got out of bed. There was no such thing as a "split soda"—or a split brandy either—in those days. We buried him in the Bay of Bengal just after a cyclone, on our way home.

By the way, the real meaning of "peg" was said to be the peg, or nail, driven into the coffin of the drinker every time he partook. And the coffin of many an Anglo-Indian of my acquaintance was all nails. A

John Collins

is simply a gin-sling with a little curaçoa in it. That is to say, soda-water, a slice of lemon, curaçoa—and gin. But by altering the proportions this can be made a very dangerous potion indeed. The officers of a certain regiment —which shall be nameless—were in the habit of putting this potion on tap, after dinner on a guest night. It was a point of honour in those evil, though poetical, times, to send no guest empty away, and more than one of those entertained by this regiment used to complain next morning at breakfast—a peg, or a swizzle, and a hot pickle sandwich—of the escape of "Private John Collins" from the regimental guard-room. For towards dawn there would not be much soda-water in that potion—which was usually served hot at that hour.

CUPS AND CORDIALS

"Can any mortal mixture
 Breathe such divine, enchanting ravishment?"

"The evil that men do lives after them."

Five recipes for claret cup—Balaclava cup—Orgeat—Ascot cup—Stout and champagne—Shandy-gaff for millionaires—Ale cup—Cobblers which will stick to the last—Home Ruler—Cherry brandy—Sloe gin—Home-made, if possible—A new industry—Apricot brandy—Highland cordial—Bitters—Jumping-powder—Orange brandy—"Mandragora"—"Sleep rock thy brain!"

I suppose there are almost as many recipes for claret cup as for a cold in the head. And of the many it is probable that the greater proportion will produce a cup which will neither cheer nor inebriate; for the simple reason that nobody, who was not inebriated already, would be physically capable of drinking enough of it. Let us first of all take the late Mr. Donald's recipe for

Claret Cup:

> A. 1 bottle claret.
> 1 wine-glassful fine pale brandy.
> ½ do. chartreuse yellow.
> ½ do. curaçoa.
> ¼ do. maraschino.
> 2 bottles soda or seltzer.[10]
> 1 lemon, cut in thin slices.
> A few sprigs of borage; not much.
> Ice and sugar to taste.

Here is a less expensive recipe:

> *B.* Put into a bowl the rind of one lemon pared very thin, add some sifted sugar, and pour over it a wine-glassful of sherry; then add a bottle of claret, more sugar to taste, a sprig of verbena, one bottle of aerated water, and a grated nutmeg; strain and ice it well.

Once more let the fact be emphasised that the better the wine, spirit, etc., the better the cup.

Here is a good cup for Ascot, when the sun is shining, and you are entertaining the fair sex.

> *C.* Put in a large bowl three bottles of claret (St. Estephe is the stamp of wine), a wine-glassful (large) of curaçoa, a pint of dry sherry, half a pint of old brandy, a large wine-glassful of raspberry syrup, three oranges and one lemon cut into slices; add a few sprigs of borage and a little cucumber rind, two bottles of seltzer water, and three bottles of Stretton water. Mix well, and sweeten. Let it stand for an hour, and then strain. Put in a large block of ice, and a few whole strawberries. Serve in small tumblers.

Another way and a simpler:

> *D.* Pour into a large jug one bottle of claret, add two wine-glassfuls of sherry, and half a glass of maraschino. Add a few sliced nectarines, or peaches, and sugar to taste (about a tablespoonful and a half). Let it stand till the sugar is dissolved, then put in a sprig of borage. Just before using add one bottle of Stretton water, and a large piece of ice.

My ideal claret cup:

> *E.* 2 bottles Pontet Canet.
>   2 wine-glassfuls old brandy.
>   1 wine-glassful curaçoa.
>   1 pint bottle sparkling moselle.
>   2 bottles aerated water.

A sprig or two of borage, and a little lemon peel.

Sugar *ad lib.*: one cup will not require much.

Add the moselle and popwater just before using; then put in a large block of ice.

Those who have never tried can have no idea of the zest which a small proportion of moselle lends to a claret cup.

My earliest recollection of a cup dates from old cricketing days beneath "Henry's holy shade," on "a match day"—as poor old "Spanky" used to phrase it; a day on which that prince of philosophers and confectioners sold his wares for cash only. Not that he had anything to do with the compounding of the

Cider Cup.

Toast a slice of bread and put it at the bottom of a large jug. Grate over the toast nearly half a small nutmeg, and a very little ginger. Add a little thin lemon rind, and six lumps of sugar. Then add two wine-glasses of sherry, and (if for adults) one of brandy. (If for boys the brandy in the sherry will suffice.) Add also the juice of a small lemon, two bottles of lively water, and (last of all) three pints of cider. Mix well, pop in a few sprigs of borage, and a block or two of ice.

Remember once more that the purer the cider the better will be the cup. There is an infinity of bad cider in the market. There used to be a prejudice against the fermented juice of the apple for all who have gouty tendencies; but as a "toe-martyr" myself, I can bear testimony to the harmlessness of the "natural" Norfolk cider made at Attleborough, in the which is no touch of Podagra.

For a good

Champagne Cup

vide Claret Cup *A*. Substituting the "sparkling" for the "ruby," the ingredients are precisely the same.

A nice, harmless beverage, suitable for a tennis party, or to accompany the "light refreshments" served at a "Cinderella" dance, or at the "breaking-up" party at a ladies' school, is

Chablis Cup.

Dissolve four or five lumps of sugar in a quarter of a pint of boiling water, and put it into a bowl with a very thin slice of lemon rind; let it stand for half-an-hour, then add a bottle of chablis, a sprig of verbena, a wine-glassful of sherry, and half-a-pint of water. Mix well, and let the mixture stand for a while, then strain, add a bottle of seltzer water, a few strawberries or raspberries, and a block of ice. Serve in small glasses.

Balaclava Cup.

> "Claret to right of 'em,
> 'Simpkin' to left of 'em—
> Cup worth a hundred!"

Get a large bowl, to represent the Valley—which only the more rabid abstainer would call the "Valley of Death." You will next require a small detachment of thin lemon rind, about two tablespoonfuls of sifted sugar, the juice of two lemons, and half a cucumber, cut into thin slices, with the peel on. Let all these ingredients skirmish about within the bowl; then bring up your heavy cavalry in the shape of two bottles of Château something, and one of the best champagne you have got. Last of all, unmask your soda-water battery; two bottles will be sufficient. Ice, and serve in tumblers.

Crimean Cup.

This is a very serious affair. So was the war. The cup, however, leads to more favourable results, and does not, like the campaign, leave a bitter taste in the mouth. Here are the ingredients:

One quart of syrup of orgeat (to make this *vide* next recipe), one pint and a half of old brandy, half a pint of maraschino, one pint of old rum, two large and one small bottles of champagne, three bottles of Seltzer-water, half-a-pound of sifted sugar, and the juice of five lemons. Peel the lemons, and put the thin rind in a mortar, with the sugar. Pound them well, and scrape the result with a silver spoon into a large bowl. Squeeze in the juice of the lemons, add the seltzer water, and stir till the sugar is quite dissolved. Then add the orgeat, and whip the mixture well with a whisk, so as to whiten it. Add the maraschino, rum, and brandy, and strain the whole into another bowl. Just before the cup is required, put in the champagne, and stir vigorously with a punch ladle. The champagne should be well iced, as no apparent ice is allowable in this mixture.

Orgeat.

Blanch and pound three-quarters of a pound of sweet almonds, and thirty bitter almonds, in one tablespoonful of water. Stir in by degrees two pints of water and three pints of milk. Strain the mixture through a cloth. Dissolve half-a-pound of loaf sugar in one pint of water. Boil and skim well, and then mix with the almond water. Add two tablespoonfuls of orange-flower water, and half-a-pint of old brandy. Be careful to boil the *eaû sucré* well, as this concoction must not be too watery.

Ascot Cup.

Odds can be laid freely on this; and the host should stay away from the temptations of the betting-ring, on purpose to make it. And—parenthetically be it observed—the man who has no soul for cup-making should never entertain at a race meeting. The servants will have other things to attend to; and even if they have not it should be remembered that a cup, or punch, like a salad, should always, if possible, be mixed by some one who is going to partake of the same.

Dissolve six ounces of sugar in half-a-pint of boiling water; add the juice of three lemons, one pint of old brandy, a wine-glassful of cherry brandy, a wine-glassful of maraschino, half a wine-glassful of yellow chartreuse, two bottles of champagne. All these should be mixed in a large silver bowl. Add a few sprigs of borage, a few slices of lemon, half-a-dozen strawberries, half-a-dozen brandied cherries, and three bottles of seltzer water. Put the bowl, having first covered it over, into the refrigerator for one hour, and before serving, put a small iceberg into the mixture, which should be served in little tumblers.

How many people, I wonder, are aware that

Champagne and Guinness' Stout

make one of the best combinations possible? You may search the wide wide world for a cookery book which will give this information; but the mixture is both grateful and strengthening, and is, moreover, far to be preferred to what is known as

Rich Man's Shandy Gaff,

which is a mixture of champagne and ale. The old Irishman said that the "blackgyard" should never be placed atop of the "gintleman," intending to convey the advice that ale should not be placed on the top of champagne. But the "black draught" indicated just above is well worth attention. It should be drunk out of a pewter tankard, and is specially recommended as a between-the-acts refresher for the amateur actor.

Ale Cup.

Squeeze the juice of a lemon into a round of hot toast; lay on it a thin piece of the rind, a tablespoonful of pounded sugar, a little grated nutmeg, and a sprig of balm. Pour over these one glass of brandy, two glasses of sherry, and three pints of mild ale. Do not allow the balm to remain in the mixture many minutes.

One of the daintiest of beverages is a

Moselle Cup.

Ingredients: One bottle of moselle. One glass of brandy. Four or five thin slices of pine-apple. The peel of half a lemon, cut very thin. Ice; and sugar *ad lib*. Just before using add one bottle of sparkling water.

Sherry Cobbler

although a popular drink in America, is but little known on this side of the Atlantic. Place in a soda-water tumbler two wine-glassfuls of sherry, one tablespoonful of sifted sugar, and two or three slices of orange. Fill the tumbler with crushed ice, and shake well. Drink through straws.

Champagne Cobbler.

Put into a large tumbler one tablespoonful of sifted sugar, with a thin paring of lemon and orange peel; fill the tumbler one-third full of crushed ice, and the remainder with champagne. Shake, and ornament with a slice of lemon, and a strawberry or two. Drink through straws.

Home Ruler.

This was a favourite drink at the bars of the House of Commons, during the reign of the Uncrowned King. It was concocted of the yolks of two raw eggs, well beaten, a little sugar added, then a tumbler of hot milk taken gradually into the mixture, and last of all a large wine-glassful of "J.J." whisky.

Cordials.

In treating of cordials, it is most advisable that they be *home made*. The bulk of the cherry brandy, ginger brandy, etc., which is sold over the counter is made with inferior brandy; and frequently the operation of blending the virtue of the fruit with the spirit has been hurried.

We will commence with the discussion of the favourite cordial of all,

Cherry Brandy.

This can either be made from Black Gean cherries, or Morellas, but the latter are better for the purpose. Every pound of cherries will require one quarter of a pound of white sugar, and one pint of the best brandy. The cherries, with the sugar well mixed with them, should be placed in wide-mouthed bottles, filled up with brandy; and if the fruit be previously pricked, the mixture will be ready in a month. But a better blend is procured if the cherries are untouched, and this principle holds good with all fruit treated in this way, and left corked for at least three months.

Sloe Gin.

For years the sloe, which is the fruit of the black-thorn, was used in England for no other purpose than the manufacture of British Port. But at this end of the nineteenth century, the public have been, and are, taking kindly to the cordial, which for a long time had been despised as an "auld wife's drink." As a matter of fact, it is just as tasty, and almost as luscious as cherry brandy. But since sloe gin became fashionable, it has become almost impossible for dwellers within twenty or thirty miles of London to make the cordial at home. For sloes fetch something like sixpence or sevenpence a pound in the market; and in consequence the hedgerows are "raided" by the (otherwise) unemployed, the fruit being usually picked before the proper time, *i.e.* when the frost has been on it. The manufacture of sloe gin is as simple as that of cherry brandy.

> All that is necessary to be done is to allow 1 lb. of sugar (white) to 1 lb. of sloes. Half fill a bottle—which need not necessarily be a wide-mouthed one—with sugared fruit, and "top up" with gin. If the sloes have been pricked, the liquor will be ready for use in two or three months; but *do not hurry it.*

In a year's time the gin will have eaten all the goodness out of the unpricked fruit, and it is in this gradual blending that the secret (as before observed) of making these cordials lies. As a rule, if you call for sloe gin at a licensed house of entertainment, you will get a ruby-coloured liquid, tasting principally of gin—and not good gin "at that." This is because the making has been hurried. Properly matured sloe gin should be the colour of full-bodied port wine.

Apricot Brandy.

> This is a cordial which is but seldom met with in this country. To every pound of fruit (which should not be quite ripe) allow one pound of loaf sugar. Put the apricots into a preserving-pan, with sufficient water to cover them. Let them boil up, and then simmer gently until tender. Remove the skins. Clarify and boil the sugar, then pour it over the fruit. Let it remain twenty-four hours. Then put the apricots into wide-mouthed bottles, and fill them up with syrup and brandy, half and half. Cork them tightly, with the tops of corks sealed. This apricot brandy

should be prepared in the month of July, and kept twelve months before using.

Highland Cordial.

Here is another rare old recipe. Ingredients, one pint of white currants, stripped of their stalks, the thin rind of a lemon, one teaspoonful of essence of ginger, and one bottle of old Scotch whisky. Let the mixture stand for forty-eight hours, and then strain through a hair sieve. Add one pound of loaf sugar, which will take at least a day to thoroughly dissolve. Then bottle off, and cork well. It will be ready for use in three months, but will keep longer.

Bitters.

One ounce of Seville orange-peel, half an ounce of gentian root, a quarter of an ounce of cardamoms. Husk the cardamoms, and crush them with the gentian root. Put them in a wide-mouthed bottle, and cover with brandy or whisky. Let the mixture remain for twelve days, then strain, and bottle off for use, after adding one ounce of lavender drops.

Ginger Brandy.

Bruise slightly two pounds of black currants, and mix them with one ounce and a half of ground ginger. Pour over them one bottle and a half of best brandy, and let the mixture stand for two days. Strain off the liquid, and add one pound of loaf sugar which has been boiled to a syrup in a little water. Bottle and cork closely.

"Jumping Powder"

comes in very handy, on a raw morning, after you have ridden a dozen miles or so to a lawn meet. "No breakfast, thanks, just a wee nip, that's all." And the ever ready butler hands round the tray. If you are wise, you will declare on

Orange Brandy

which, as a rule, is well worth sampling, in a house important enough to entertain hunting men. And orange brandy "goes" much better than any other liqueur, or cordial, before noon.

It should be made in the month of March. Take the thin rinds of six Seville oranges, and put them into a stone jar, with half-a-pint of the strained juice, and two quarts of good old brandy. Let it remain three days, then add one pound and a quarter of loaf sugar—broken, not pounded—and stir till the sugar is dissolved. Let the liquor stand a day, strain it through paper till quite clear, pour into bottles, and cork tightly. The longer it is kept the better.

Mandragora.

"Can't sleep." Eh? What! not after a dry chapter on liquids? Drink this, and you will not require any rocking.

Simmer half-a-pint of old ale, and just as it is about to boil pour it into a tumbler, grate a little nutmeg over it, and add a teaspoonful of moist sugar, and two tablespoonfuls of brandy. Good night, Hamlet!

THE DAYLIGHT DRINK

"Something too much of this."

"A nipping and an eager air."

Evil effects of dram-drinking—The "Gin-crawl"—Abstinence in H.M. service—City manners and customs—Useless to argue with the soaker—Cocktails—Pet names for drams—The free lunch system—Fancy mixtures—Why no Cassis?—Good advice like water on a duck's back.

Whilst holding the same opinion as the epicure who declared that good eating required good drinking, there is no question but that there should be a limit to both. There is, as Shakespeare told us, a tide in the affairs of man, so why should there not be in this particular affair? Why should it be only ebb tide during the few hours that the man is wrapped in the arms of a Bacchanalian Morpheus, either in bed or in custody? The abuse of good liquor is surely as criminal a folly as the abstention therefrom; and the man who mixes his liquors injudiciously lacks that refinement of taste and understanding which is necessary for the appreciation of a good deal of this book, or indeed of any other useful volume. Our grandfathers swore terribly, and drank deep; but their fun did not commence until after dinner. And they drank, for the most part, the best of ale, and such port wine as is not to be had in these days of free trade (which is only an euphemism for adulteration) and motor cars. Although mine own teeth are, periodically, set on edge by the juice of the grape consumed by an ancestor or two; although the gout within me is an heritage from the three-, aye! and four-, bottle era, I respect mine ancestors, in that they knew not "gin and bitters." The baleful habit of alcoholising the inner sinner between meal times, the pernicious habit of dram-drinking, or "nipping," from early morn till dewy eve, was not introduced into our cities until the latter half of the nineteenth century had set in. "Brandy-and-soda," at first only used as a "livener"—and a deadly livener it is—was unknown during the early Victorian era; and the "gin-crawl," that interminable slouch around the hostelries, is a rank growth of modernity.

The "nipping habit" came to us, with other pernicious "notions," from across the Atlantic Ocean. It was Brother Jonathan who established the bar system; and although for the most part, throughout Great Britain, the alcohol is dispensed by young ladies with fine eyes and a great deal of adventitious hair, and the "bar-keep," with his big watch chain, and his "guns," placed within easy reach, for quick-shooting saloon practice, is unknown on this side, the hurt of the system (to employ an Americanism) "gets there just the same." There is not the same amount of carousing in the British army as in the days when I was a "gilded popinjay" (in the language of Mr. John Burns; "a five-and-twopenny assassin," in the words of somebody else). In those days the use of alcohol, if not absolutely encouraged for the use of the subaltern, was winked at by his superiors, as long as the subalterns were not on duty, or on the line of march—and I don't know so much about the line of march, either. But with any orderly or responsible duty to be done, the beverage of heroes was not admired. "Now mind," once observed our revered colonel, in the ante-room, after dinner, "none of you young officers get seeing snakes and things, or otherwise rendering yourselves unfit for service; or I'll try the lot of you by court martial, I will, by ——." Here the adjutant let the regimental bible drop with a bang. Tea is the favourite ante-room refreshment nowadays, when the officer, young or old, is always either on duty, or at school. And the education of the modern warrior is never completed.

But the civilian—sing ho! the wicked civilian—is a reveller, and a winebibber, for the most part. Very little business is transacted except over what is called "a friendly glass." "I want seven hundred an' forty-five from you, old chappie," says Reggie de Beers of the "House," on settling day. "Right," replies his friend young "Berthas": "toss you double or quits. Down with it!" And it would be a cold day were not a magnum or two of "the Boy" to be opened over the transaction. The cheap eating-house keeper who has spent his morning at the "market," cheapening a couple of pigs, or a dozen scraggy fowls, will have spent double the money he has saved in the bargain, in rum and six-penny ale, ere he gets home again; and even a wholesale deal in evening journals, between two youths in the street, requires to be "wetted." Very sad is it not? But, as anything which I—who am popularly supposed to be something resembling a roysterer, but who am in reality one of the most discreet of those who enjoy life—can write is not likely to work a change in the system which obtains amongst English-speaking nations, perhaps the sooner I get on with the programme the better. Later on I may revert to the subject.

Amongst daylight (and midnight, for the matter of that) drinks, the COCKTAIL, that fascinating importation from Dollarland, holds a prominent place. This is a concoction for which, with American bars all over the Metropolis, the cockney does not really require any recipe. But as I trust to have some country readers, a few directions may be appended.

Brandy Cocktail.

One wine-glassful of old brandy, six drops of Angostura bitters, and twenty drops of curaçoa, in a small tumbler—all cocktails should be made in a small silver tumbler—shake, and pour into glass tumbler, then fill up with crushed ice. Put a shred of lemon peel atop.

Champagne Cocktail.

One teaspoonful of sifted sugar, ten drops of Angostura bitters, a small slice of pine-apple, and a shred of lemon peel. Strain into glass tumbler, add crushed ice, and as much champagne as the tumbler will hold. Mix with a spoon.

Bengal Cocktail.

Fill tumbler half full of crushed ice. Add thirty drops of maraschino, one tablespoonful of pine-apple syrup, thirty drops of curaçoa, six drops of Angostura bitters, one wine-glassful of old brandy. Stir, and put a shred of lemon peel atop.

Milford Cocktail.

(Dedicated to Mr. Jersey.)

Put into a half-pint tumbler a couple of lumps of best ice, one teaspoonful of sifted sugar, one teaspoonful of orange bitters, half a wine-glassful of brandy. Top up with bottled cider, and mix with a spoon. Serve with a strawberry, and a sprig of verbena atop.

Manhattan Cocktail.

Half a wine-glassful of vermouth (Italian), half a wine-glassful of rye whisky (according to the American recipe, though, personally, I prefer Scotch), ten drops of Angostura bitters, and six drops of curaçoa. Add ice, shake well, and strain. Put a shred of lemon peel atop.

Yum Yum Cocktail.

Break the yolk of a new-laid egg into a small tumbler, and put a teaspoonful of sugar on it. Then six drops of Angostura bitters, a wine-glassful of sherry, and half a wine-glassful of brandy. Shake all well together, and strain. Dust a very little cinnamon over the top.

Gin Cocktail.

Ten drops of Angostura bitters, one wine-glassful of gin, ten drops of curaçoa, one shred of lemon peel. Fill up with ice, shake, and strain.

Newport Cocktail.

Put two lumps of ice and a small *slice* of lemon into the tumbler, add six drops of Angostura bitters, half a wine-glassful of noyau, and a wine-glassful of brandy. Stir well, and serve with peel atop.

Saratoga Cocktail.

This is a more important affair, and requires a large tumbler for the initial stage. One teaspoonful of pine-apple syrup, ten drops of

Angostura bitters, one teaspoonful of maraschino, and a wine-glassful of old brandy. Nearly fill the tumbler with crushed ice, and shake well. Then place a couple of strawberries in a small tumbler, strain the liquid on them, put in a strip of lemon peel, and top up with champagne.

Whisky Cocktail.

Put into a small tumbler ten drops of Angostura bitters, and one wine-glassful of Scotch whisky. Fill the tumbler with crushed ice, shake well, strain into a large wine-glass, and place a strip of peel atop.

But the ordinary British "bar-cuddler"—as he is called in the slang of the day—recks not of cocktails, nor, indeed, of Columbian combinations of any sort. He has his own particular "vanity," and frequently a pet name for it. "Gin-and-angry-story" (Angostura), "slow-and-old" (sloe-gin and Old Tom), "pony o' Burton, please miss," are a few of the demands the attentive listener may hear given. Orange-gin, gin-and-orange-gin, gin-and-sherry (O bile where is thy sting?), are favourite midday "refreshers"; and I have heard a well-known barrister call for "a split Worcester" (a small wine-glassful of Worcester sauce with a split soda), without a smile on his expressive countenance. "Small lem. and a dash" is a favourite summer beverage, and, withal, a harmless one, consisting of a small bottle of lemonade with about an eighth of a pint of bitter ale added thereto. In one old-fashioned hostelry I wot of—the same in which the chair of the late Doctor Samuel Johnson is on view—customers who require to be stimulated with gin call for "rack," and Irish whisky is known by none other name than "Cork." The habitual "bar-cuddler" usually rubs his hands violently together, as he requests a little attention from the presiding Hebe; and affects a sort of shocked surprise at the presence on the scene of any one of his friends or acquaintances. He is well-up, too, in the slang phraseology of the day, which he will ride to death on every available opportunity. Full well do I remember him in the "How's your poor feet?" era; and it seems but yesterday that he was informing the company in assertive tones, "Now we *shan't* be long!" The "free lunch" idea of the Yankees is only thoroughly carried out in the "North Countree," where, at the best hotels, there is often a great bowl of soup, or a dish of jugged hare, or of Irish stew, *pro bono publico*; and by *publico* is implied the hotel directorate as well as the customers. In London, however, the free lunch seldom soars above salted almonds, coffee beans, cloves, with biscuits and American cheese. But at most refreshment-houses is to be obtained for cash some sort of a restorative sandwich, or *bonne bouche,* in the which anchovies and hard-boiled eggs play leading parts; and amongst other restorative food, I have noticed that parallelograms of cold Welsh rarebit are exceedingly popular amongst wine-travellers and advertisement-agents. The genius who propounded the statement that "there is nothing like leather" could surely never have sampled a cold Welsh rarebit!

Bosom Caresser.

Put into a small tumbler one wine-glassful of sherry, half a wine-glassful of old brandy, the yolk of an egg, two teaspoonfuls of sugar, and two grains of cayenne pepper; add crushed ice, shake well, strain, and dust over with nutmeg and cinnamon.

A Nicobine,

(or "Knickerbein" as I have seen it spelt), used to be a favourite "short" drink in Malta, and consisted of the yolk of an egg (intact) in a wine-glass with *layers* of curaçoa, maraschino, and green chartreuse; the liquors not allowed to mix with one another. The "knickerbein" recipe differs materially from this, as brandy is substituted for chartreuse, and the ingredients are shaken up and strained, the white of the egg being whisked and placed atop. But, either way, you will get a good, bile-provoking mixture. In the

West Indies,

if you thirst for a rum and milk, cocoa-nut milk is the "only wear"; and a very delicious potion it is. A favourite mixture in Jamaica was the juice of a "star" apple, the juice of an orange, a wine-glassful of sherry, and a dust of nutmeg. I never heard a name given to this.

Bull's Milk.

This is a comforting drink for summer or winter. During the latter season, instead of adding ice, the mixture may be heated.

One teaspoonful of sugar in a *large* tumbler, half-a-pint of milk, half a wine-glassful of rum, a wine-glassful of brandy; add ice, shake well, strain, and powder with cinnamon and nutmeg.

Fairy Kiss.

Put into a small tumbler the juice of a quarter of lemon, a quarter of a wine-glassful each of the following:—Vanilla syrup, curaçoa, yellow chartreuse, brandy. Add ice, shake, and strain.

Flash of Lightning.

One-third of a wine-glassful each of the following, in a small tumbler:—Raspberry syrup, curaçoa, brandy, and three drops of Angostura bitters. Add ice, shake and strain.

Flip Flap.

One wine-glassful of milk in a small tumbler, one well-beaten egg, a little sugar, and a wine-glassful of port. Ice, shake, strain, and sprinkle with cinnamon and nutmeg.

Maiden's Blush.

Half a wine-glassful of sherry in a small tumbler, a quarter of a wine-glassful of strawberry syrup, and a little lemon juice. Add ice, and a little raspberry syrup. Shake, and drink through straws.

Athole Brose

is compounded, according to a favourite author, in the following manner:—

"Upon virgin honeycombs you pour, according to their amount, the oldest French brandy and the most indisputable Scotch whisky in equal proportions. You allow this goodly mixture to stand for days in a large pipkin in a cool place, and it is then strained and ready for drinking. Epicures drop into the jug, by way of imparting artistic finish, a small fragment of the honeycomb itself. This I deprecate."

Tiger's Milk.

Small tumbler. Half a wine-glassful each of cider and Irish whisky, a wine-glassful of peach brandy. Beat up separately the white of an egg with a little sugar, and add this. Fill up the tumbler with ice; shake, and strain. Add half a tumbler of milk, and grate a little nutmeg atop.

Wyndham.

Large tumbler. Equal quantities (a liqueur glass of each) of maraschino, curaçoa, brandy, with a little orange peel, and sugar. Add a glass of champagne, and a *small* bottle of seltzer water. Ice, and mix well together. Stir with a spoon.

Happy Eliza.

Put into a skillet twelve fresh dried figs cut open, four apples cut into slices without peeling, and half a pound of loaf sugar, broken small. Add two quarts of water, boil for twenty minutes, strain through a— where's the brandy? Stop! I've turned over two leaves, and got amongst the *Temperance Drinks*. Rein back!

Mint Julep.

This, properly made, is the most delicious of all American beverages. It is mixed in a large tumbler, in the which are placed, first of all, two and a half tablespoonfuls of water, one tablespoonful of sugar (crushed), and two or three sprigs of mint, which should be pressed, with a spoon or crusher, into the sugar and water to extract the flavour.

Add two wine-glassfuls of old brandy—*now* we shan't be long—fill up with powdered ice, shake well, get the mint to the top of the tumbler, stalks down, and put a few strawberries and slices of orange atop. Shake in a little rum, last of all, and drink through straws.

Possets.

(An eighteenth-century recipe.)

"Take three gills of sweet cream, a grated rind of lemon, and juice thereof, three-quarters of a pint of sack or Rhenish wine. Sweeten to your taste with loaf sugar, then beat in a bowl with a whisk for one hour, and fill your glasses and drink to the king."

We are tolerably loyal in this our time; still it is problematical if there exist man or woman in Merry England, in our day who would whisk a mixture for sixty minutes by the clock, even with the prospect of drinking to the reigning monarch.

Brandy Sour.

This is simplicity itself. A teaspoonful of sifted sugar in a small tumbler, a little lemon rind and juice, one wine-glassful of brandy. Fill nearly up with crushed ice, shake and strain. WHISKY SOUR is merely Scotch whisky treated in the same kind, open-handed manner, with the addition of a few drops of raspberry syrup.

Blue Blazer.

Don't be frightened; there is absolutely no danger. Put into a silver mug, or jug, previously heated, two wine-glassfuls of overproof (or proof) Scotch whisky, and one wine-glassful of *boiling* water. Set the liquor on fire, and pass the blazing liquor into another mug, also well heated. Pass to and fro, and serve in a tumbler, with a lump of sugar and a little thin lemon peel. Be very particular not to drop any of the blazer on the cat, or the hearth-rug, or the youngest child. This drink would, I should think, have satisfied the aspirations of Mr. Daniel Quilp.

One of the most wholesome of all "refreshers," is a simple liquor, distilled from black-currants, and known to our lively neighbours as

Cassis.

This syrup can be obtained in the humblest *cabaret* in France; but we have to thank the eccentric and illogical ways of our Customs Department for its absence from most of our own wine lists. The duty is so prohibitive—being half as much again as that levied on French brandy—that it would pay nobody but said Customs Department to import it into England; and yet the amount of alcohol contained in cassis is infinitesimal. Strange to say nobody has ever started a cassis still on this side. One would imagine that the process would be simplicity itself; as the liquor is nothing but cold black-currant tea, with a suspicion of alcohol in it.

Sligo Slop.

This is an Irish delight. The juice of ten lemons, strained, ten tablespoonfuls of sifted sugar, one quart of John Jameson's oldest and best whisky, and two port wine-glassfuls of curaçoa, all mixed together. Let the mixture stand for a day or two, and then bottle. This should be drunk neat, in liqueur-glasses, and is said to be most effectual "jumping-powder." It certainly reads conducive to timber-topping.

Take it altogether the daylight drink is a mistake. It is simply ruin to appetite; it is more expensive than those who indulge therein are aware of at the time. It ruins the nerves, sooner or later; it is *not* conducive to business, unless for those whose heads are especially hard; and it spoils the palate for the good wine which is poured forth later on. The precept cannot be too widely laid down, too fully known:

Do not drink between Meals!

GASTRONOMY IN FICTION AND DRAMA

"Let me not burst in ignorance."

"A chiel's amang ye, taking notes."

Thomas Carlyle—Thackeray—Harrison Ainsworth—Sir Walter Scott—Miss Braddon—Marie Corelli—F. C. Philips—Blackmore—Charles Dickens—*Pickwick* reeking with alcohol—Brandy and oysters—*Little Dorrit*—*Great Expectations*—Micawber as a punch-maker—*David Copperfield*—"Practicable" food on the stage—"Johnny" Toole's story of Tiny Tim and the goose.

Considering the number of books which have been published during the nineteenth century, it is astonishing how few of them deal with eating and drinking. We read of a banquet or two, certainly, in the works of the divine William, but no particulars as to the *cuisine* are entered into. "Cold Banquo" hardly sounds appetising. Thomas Carlyle was a notorious dyspeptic, so it is no cause for wonderment that he did not bequeath to posterity the recipes for a dainty dish or two, or a good Derby Day "Cup." Thackeray understood but little about cookery, nor was Whyte Melville much better versed in the mysteries of the kitchen. Harrison Ainsworth touched lightly on gastronomy occasionally, whilst Charles Lamb, Sydney Smith, and others (blessings light on the man who invented the phrase "and others") delighted therein. Miss Braddon has slurred it over hitherto, and Marie Corelli scorns all mention of any refreshment but absinthe—a weird liquid which is altogether absent from these pages. In the lighter novels of Mr. F. C. Philips, there is but little mention of solid food except devilled caviare, which sounds nasty; but most of Mr. Philips's men, and all his women, drink to excess—principally champagne, brandy, and green chartreuse. And one of his heroines is a firm believer in the merits of cognac as a "settler" of champagne.

According to Mr. R. D. Blackmore, the natives of Exmoor did themselves particularly well, in the seventeenth century. In that most delightful romance *Lorna Doone* is a description of a meal set before Tom Faggus, the celebrated highwayman, by the Ridd family, at Plover's Barrows:—

"A few oysters first, and then dried salmon, and then ham and eggs, done in small curled rashers, and then a few collops of venison toasted, and next a little cold roast pig, and a woodcock on toast to finish with."

This meal was washed down with home-brewed ale, followed by Schiedam and hot water.

One man, and one man alone, who has left his name printed deep on the sands of time as a writer, thoroughly revelled in the mighty subjects of eating and drinking. Need his name be mentioned? What is, after all, the great secret of the popularity of

Charles Dickens

as a novelist? His broad, generous views on the subject of meals, as expressed through the mouths of most of the characters in his works; as also the homely nature of such meals, and the good and great deeds to which they led. I once laid myself out to count the number of times that alcoholic refreshment is mentioned in some of the principal works of the great author; and the record, for *Pickwick* alone, was sufficient to sweep from the surface of the earth, with its fiery breath, the entire Blue Ribbon Army. Mr. Pickwick was what would be called nowadays a "moderate drinker." That is to say, he seldom neglected an "excuse for a lotion," nor did he despise the "daylight drink." But we only read of his being overcome by his potations on two occasions; after the cricket dinner at Muggleton, and after the shooting luncheon on Captain Boldwig's ground. And upon the latter occasion I am convinced that the hot sun had far more to do with his temporary obfuscation than the cold punch. Bob Sawyer and Ben Allen were by no means exaggerated types of the medical students of the time. The "deputy sawbones" of to-day writes pamphlets, drinks coffee, and pays his landlady every Saturday. And it was a happy touch of Dickens to make Sawyer and Allen eat oysters, and wash them down with neat brandy, before breakfast. I have known medical students, aye! and full-blown surgeons too, who would commit equally daring acts; although I doubt much if they would have shone at the breakfast-table afterwards, or on the ice later in the day. For the effect exercised by brandy on oysters is pretty well known to science.

Breathes there a man with soul so dead as not to appreciate the delights of Dingley Dell? Free trade and other horrors have combined to crush the British yeoman of to-day; but we none the less delight to read of him as he was, and I do not know a better cure for an attack of "blue devils"—or should it be "black dog?"—than a good dose of Dingley Dell. The wholesale manner in which Mr. Wardle takes possession of the Pickwickians—only one of whom he knows intimately—for purposes of entertainment, is especially delightful, and worthy of imitation; and I can only regret the absence of a good, cunningly-mixed "cup" at the picnic after the Chatham review. The wine drunk at this picnic would seem to have been sherry; as there was not such a glut of "the sparkling" in those good old times. And the prompt way in which "Emma" is commanded to "bring out the cherry brandy," before his guests have been two minutes in the house, bespeaks the character of dear old Wardle in once. "The Leathern Bottle," a charming old-world hostelry in that picturesque country lying between Rochester and Cobham, would hardly have been in existence now, let alone doing a roaring trade, but for the publication of *Pickwick*; and the notion of the obese Tupman solacing himself for blighted hopes and taking his leave of the world on a diet of roast fowl bacon, ale, etc., is unique. The bill-of-fare at the aforementioned shooting luncheon might not, perhaps, satisfy the aspirations of Sir Mota Kerr, or some other *nouveau riche* of to-day, but there was plenty to eat and drink. Here is the list, in Mr. Samuel Weller's own words:

"Weal pie, tongue: a wery good thing when it ain't a woman's: bread, knuckle o' ham, reg'lar picter, cold beef in slices; wery good. What's in them stone jars, young touch-and-go?"

"Beer in this one," replied the boy, taking from his shoulder a couple of large stone bottles, fastened together by a leathern strap, "cold punch in t'other."

"And a wery good notion of a lunch it is, take it altogether," said Mr. Weller.

Possibly; though cold beef in slices would be apt to get rather dryer than was desirable on a warm day. And milk punch hardly seems the sort of tipple to encourage accuracy of aim.

Mrs. Bardell's notion of a nice little supper we gather from the same immortal work, was "a couple of sets of pettitoes and some toasted cheese." The pettitoes were presumably simmered in milk, and the cheese was, undoubtedly, "browning away most delightfully in a little Dutch oven in front of the fire." Most of us will smack our lips after this description; though details are lacking as to the contents of the "black bottle" which was produced from "a small closet." But amongst students of *Pickwick*, "Old Tom" is a hot favourite.

The Deputy Shepherd's particular "vanity" appears to have been buttered toast and reeking hot pine-apple rum and water, which sounds like swimming-in-the-head; and going straight through the book, we next pause at the description of the supper given by the medical students, at their lodgings in the Borough, to the Pickwickians.

"The man to whom the order for the oysters had been sent had not been told to open them; it is a very difficult thing to open an oyster with a limp knife or a two-pronged fork; and very little was done in this way. Very little of the beef was done either; and the ham (which was from the German-sausage shop round the corner) was in a similar predicament. However, there was plenty of porter in a tin can; and the cheese went a great way, for it was very strong."

Probably the oysters had not been paid for in advance, and the man imagined that they would be returned upon his hands none the worse. For at that time—as has been remarked before, in this volume on gastronomy—the knowledge that an oyster baked in his own shells, in the middle of a clear fire, is an appetising dish, does not appear to have been universal.

It is questionable if a supper consisting of a boiled leg of mutton "with the usual trimmings" would have satisfied the taste of the "gentleman's gentleman" of to-day, who is a hypercritic, if anything; but let that supper be taken as read. Also let it be noted that the appetite of the redoubtable

Pickwick never seems to have failed him, even in the sponging-house—five to one can be betted that those chops were *fried*—or in the Fleet Prison itself. And mention of this establishment recalls the extravagant folly of Job Trotter (who of all men ought to have known better) in purchasing "a small piece of raw loin of mutton" for the refection of himself and ruined master; when for the same money he could surely have obtained a sufficiency of bullock's cheek or liver, potatoes, and onions, to provide dinner for three days. *Vide* the "Kent Road Cookery," in one of my earlier chapters. The description of the journeys from Bristol to Birmingham, and back to London, absolutely reeks with food and alcohol; and it has always smacked of the mysterious to myself how Sam Weller, a pure Cockney, could have known so much of the capacities of the various hostelries on the road. Evidently his knowledge of other places besides London was "peculiar." Last scene of all in *Pickwick* requiring mention here, is the refection given to Mr. Solomon Pell in honour of the proving of the late Dame Weller's last will and testament. "Porter, cold beef, and oysters," were some of the incidents of that meal, and we read that "the coachman with the hoarse voice took an imperial pint of vinegar with his oysters, without betraying the least emotion."

It is also set down that brandy and water, as usual in this history, followed the oysters; but we are not told if any of those coachmen ever handled the ribbons again, or if Mr. Solomon Pell spent his declining days in the infirmary.

In fact, there are not many chapters in Charles Dickens' works in which the knife and fork do not play prominent parts. The food is, for the most part, simple and homely; the seed sown in England by the fairy *Ala* had hardly begun to germinate at the time the novels were written. Still there is, naturally, a suspicion of *Ala* at the very commencement of *Little Dorrit*, the scene being laid in the Marseilles prison, where Monsieur Rigaud feasts off Lyons sausage, veal in savoury jelly, white bread, strachino cheese, and good claret, the while his humble companion, Signor John Baptist, has to content himself with stale bread, through reverses at gambling with his fellow prisoner. After that, there is no mention of a "square meal" until we get to Mr. Casby's, the "Patriarch." "Everything about the patriarchal household," we are told, "promoted quiet digestion"; and the dinner mentioned began with "some soup, some fried soles, a butter-boat of shrimp sauce, and a dish of potatoes." Rare old Casby! "Mutton, a steak, and an apple pie"—and presumably cheese—furnished the more solid portion of the banquet, which appears to have been washed down with porter and sherry wine, and enlivened by the inconsequent remarks of "Mr. F.'s Aunt."

In *Great Expectations* occurs the celebrated banquet at the Chateau Gargery on Christmas Day, consisting of a leg of pickled pork and greens, a pair of roast stuffed fowls, a handsome mince pie, and a plum-pudding. The absence of the savoury pork-pie, and the presence of tar-water in the brandy are incidents at that banquet familiar enough to Sir Frank Lockwood, Q.C., M.P., and other close students of Dickens, whose favourite dinner-dish would appear to have been a fowl, stuffed or otherwise, roast or boiled.

In *Oliver Twist* we get casual mention of oysters, sheep's heads, and a rabbit pie, with plenty of alcohol; but the bill of fare, on the whole, is not an appetising one. The meat and drink at the Maypole Hotel, in *Barnaby Rudge*, would appear to have been deservedly popular; and the description of Gabriel Varden's breakfast is calculated to bring water to the most callous mouth:

"Over and above the ordinary tea equipage the board creaked beneath the weight of a jolly round of beef, a ham of the first magnitude, and sundry towers of buttered Yorkshire cake, piled slice upon slice in most alluring order. There was also a goodly jug of well-browned clay, fashioned into the form of an old gentleman not by any means unlike the locksmith, atop of whose bald head was a fine white froth answering to his wig, indicative, beyond dispute, of sparkling home brewed ale. But better than fair home-brewed, or Yorkshire cake, or ham, or beef, or anything to eat or drink that earth or air or water can supply, there sat, presiding over all, the locksmith's rosy daughter, before whose dark eyes even beef grew insignificant, and malt became as nothing."

Ah-h-h!

There is not much eating in *A Tale of Two Cities*; but an intolerable amount of assorted "sack." In *Sketches by Boz* we learn that Dickens had no great opinion of public dinners, and that oysters were, at that period, occasionally opened by the fair sex. There is a nice flavour of fowl and old Madeira about *Dombey and Son*, and the description of the dinner at Doctor Blimber's establishment for young gentlemen is worth requoting:

"There was some nice soup; also roast meat, boiled meat, vegetables, pie, and cheese." [*Cheese* at a small boys' school!] "Every young gentleman had a massive silver fork and a napkin; and all the arrangements were stately and handsome. In particular there was a butler in a blue coat and bright buttons" [surely this was a footman?] "who gave quite a winey flavour to the table beer, he poured it out so superbly."

Dinner at Mrs. Jellyby's in *Bleak House* is one of the funniest and most delightful incidents in the book, especially the attendance. "The young woman with the flannel bandage waited, and dropped everything on the table wherever it happened to go, and never moved it again until she put it on the stairs. The person I had seen in pattens (who I suppose to have been the cook) frequently came and skirmished with her at the door, and there appeared to be ill-will between them." The dinner given by Mr. Guppy at the "Slap Bang" dining house is another feature of this book—veal and ham, and French beans, summer cabbage, pots of half-and-half, marrow puddings, "three Cheshires" and "three small rums." Of the items in this list, the marrow pudding seems to be as extinct—in London, at all events—as the dodo. It appears to be a mixture of bread, pounded almonds, cream, eggs, lemon peel, sugar, nutmeg, and marrow; and sounds nice.

David Copperfield's dinner in his Buckingham Street chambers was an event with a disastrous termination. "It was a remarkable want of forethought on the part of the ironmonger who had made Mrs. Crupp's kitchen fireplace, that it was capable of cooking nothing but chops and mashed potatoes. As to a fish-kettle, Mrs. Crupp said 'Well! would I only come and look at the range? She couldn't say fairer than that. Would I come and look at it?' As I should not have been much the wiser if I *had* looked at it I said never mind fish. But Mrs. Crupp said, 'Don't say that; oysters was in, and why not them?' So *that* was settled. Mrs. Crupp then said 'What she would recommend would be this. A pair of hot roast fowls—from the pastry cook's; a dish of stewed beef, with vegetables—from the pastry cook's; two little corner things, as a raised pie and a dish of kidneys—from the pastry cook's; a tart, and (if I liked) a shape of jelly—from the pastry cook's. This,' Mrs. Crupp said, 'would leave her at full liberty to concentrate her mind on the potatoes, and to serve up the cheese and celery as she could wish to see it done.'"

Then blessings on thee, Micawber, most charming of characters in fiction, mightiest of punch-brewers! The only fault I have to find with the novel of *David Copperfield* is that we don't get enough of Micawber. The same fault, however, could hardly be said to lie in the play; for if ever there was a "fat" part, it is Wilkins Micawber.

Martin Chuzzlewit bubbles over with eating and drinking; and "Todgers" has become as proverbial as Hamlet. In *Nicholas Nickleby*, too, we find plenty of mention of solids and liquids; and as a poor stroller myself at one time, it has always struck me that "business" could not have been so very bad, after all, in the Crummles Combination; for the manager, at all events, seems to have fared particularly well. Last on the list comes *The Old Curiosity Shop*, with the celebrated stew at the "Jolly Sandboys," the ingredients in which have already been quoted by the present writer. With regard to this stew all that I have to remark is that I should have substituted an ox-kidney for the tripe, and left out the "sparrowgrass," the flavour of which would be quite lost in the crowd of ingredients. But there! who can cavil at such a feast? "Fetch me a pint of warm ale, and don't let nobody bring into the room even so much as a biscuit till the time arrives."

Codlin may not have been "the friend"; but he was certainly the judge of the "Punch" party.

In this realistic age, meals on the stage have to be provided from high-class hotels or restaurants; and this is, probably, the chief reason why there is so little eating and drinking introduced into the modern drama. Gone are the nights of the banquet of pasteboard poultry, "property" pine-apples, and gilded flagons containing nothing more sustaining than the atmosphere of coal-gas. Not much faith is placed in the comic scenes of a pantomime nowadays; or it is probable that the clown would purloin real York hams, and stuff Wall's sausages into the pockets of his ample pants. Champagne is champagne under the present regime of raised prices, raised salaries, raised everything; and it is not so long since I overheard an actor-manager chide a waiter from a fashionable restaurant, for forgetting the *Soubise* sauce, when he brought the cutlets.

In my acting days we usually had canvas fowls, stuffed with sawdust, when we revelled on the stage; or, if business had been particularly good, the poultry was made from breakfast rolls, with pieces skewered on, to represent the limbs. And the potables—Gadzooks! What horrible concoctions have found their way down this unsuspecting throttle! Sherry was invariably represented by cold tea, which is palatable enough if home-made, under careful superintendence, but, drawn in the property-master's den, usually tasted of glue. Ginger beer, at three-farthings for two bottles, poured into tumblers containing portions of a seidlitz-powder, always did duty for champagne; and as for port or claret—well, I quite thought I had swallowed the deadliest of poisons one night, until assured it was only the cold leavings of the stage-door-keeper's coffee!

The story of Tiny Tim who ate the goose is a pretty familiar one in stage circles. When playing Bob Cratchit, in *The Christmas Carol* at the Adelphi, under Mr. Benjamin Webster's management, Mr. J. L. Toole had to carve a real goose and a "practicable" plum-pudding during the run of that piece, forty nights. And the little girl who played Tiny Tim used to finish her portions of goose and pudding with such amazing celerity that Mr. Toole became quite alarmed on her account.

"'I don't like it,' I said," writes dear friend "Johnny," in his *Reminiscences*; "'I can't conceive where a poor, delicate little thing like that puts the food. Besides, although I like the children to enjoy a treat'—and how they kept on enjoying it for forty nights was a mystery, for I got into such a condition that if I dined at a friend's house, and goose was on the table, I regarded it as a personal affront—I said, referring to Tiny Tim, 'I don't like greediness; and it is additionally repulsive in a refined-looking, delicate little thing like this; besides, it destroys the sentiment of the situation—and when I, as Bob, ought to feel most pathetic, I am always wondering where the goose and the pudding are, or whether anything serious in the way of a fit will happen to Tiny Tim before the audience, in consequence of her unnatural gorging!' Mrs. Mellon laughed at me at first, but eventually we decided to watch Tiny Tim together.

"We watched as well as we could, and the moment Tiny Tim was seated, and began to eat, we observed a curious shuffling movement at the stage-fireplace, and everything that I had given her, goose and potatoes, and apple-sauce disappeared behind the sham stove, the child pretending to eat as heartily as ever from the empty plate. When the performance was over, Mrs. Mellon and myself asked the little girl what became of the food she did not eat, and, after a little hesitation, she confessed that her little sister (I should mention that they were the children of one of the scene-shifters) waited on the other side of the fireplace for the supplies, and then the whole family enjoyed a hearty supper every night.

"Dickens was very much interested in the incident. When I had finished, he smiled a little sadly, I thought, and then, shaking me by the hand, he said, 'Ah! you ought to have given her the whole goose.'"

> "Raze out the written troubles of the brain,
> And with some antibilious antidote
> Cleanse the stuff'd bosom of that perilous stuff
> Which weighs upon the soul."

William of Normandy—A "head" wind at sea—Beware the druggist—Pick-me-ups of all sorts and conditions—Anchovy toast for the invalid—A small bottle—Straight talks to fanatics—Total abstinence as bad as the other thing—Moderation in all things—Wisely and slow—*Carpe diem*—But have a thought for the morrow.

"I care not," observed William of Normandy to his quartermaster-general, on the morning after the revelry which followed the Battle of Hastings, "who makes these barbarians' wines; send me the man who can remove the beehive from my o'erwrought brain."

This remark is not to be found in Macaulay's *History of England*; but learned authorities who have read the original MS. in Early Norman, make no doubt as to the correct translation.

"It is excellent," as the poet says, "to have a giant's thirst; but it is tyrannous to use it like a giant." And not only "tyrannous" but short-sighted. For the law of compensation is one of the first edicts of Nature. The same beneficent hand which provides the simple fruits of the earth for the delectation of man, furnishes also the slug and the wasp, to see that he doesn't get too much. Our friend the dog is deprived of the power of articulation, but he has a tail which can be wagged at the speed of 600 revolutions to the minute. And the man who overtaxes the powers of his inner mechanism during the hours of darkness is certain to feel the effects, to be smitten of conscience, and troubled of brain, when he awakes, a few hours later on. As this is not a medical treatise it would be out of place to analyse at length the abominable habit which the human brain and stomach have acquired, of acting and reacting on each other; suffice it to say that there is no surer sign of the weakness and helplessness of poor, frail, sinful, fallen humanity than the obstinacy with which so many of us will, for the sake of an hour or two's revelry, boldly bid for five times the amount of misery and remorse. And this more especially applies to a life on the ocean wave. The midshipmite who over-estimates his swallowing capacity is no longer "mast-headed" next morning; but the writer has experienced a cyclone in the Bay of Bengal, ere the effects of a birthday party on the previous night had been surmounted; and the effects of "mast-heading" could hardly have been less desirable. In that most delightful work for the young, Dana's *Two years before the Mast*, we read:

"Our forecastle, as usual after a liberty-day, was a scene of tumult all night long, from the drunken ones. They had just got to sleep toward morning, when they were turned up with the rest, and kept at work all day in the water, carrying hides, their heads aching so that they could hardly stand. This is sailors' pleasure."

Dana himself was ordered up aloft, to reef "torpsles," on his first morning at sea; and he had probably had some sort of a farewell carouse, 'ere quitting Boston. And the present writer upon one occasion—such is the irony of fate—was told off to indite a leading article on "Temperance" for an evening journal, within a very few hours of the termination of a "Derby" banquet.

But how shall we alleviate the pangs? How make that dreadful "day after" endurable enough to cause us to offer up thanks for being still allowed to live? Come, the panacea, good doctor!

First of all, then, avoid the chemist and his works. I mean no disrespect to my good friend Sainsbury, or his "Number One Pick-me-up," whose corpse-reviving claims are indisputable; but at the same time the habitual swallower of drugs does not lead the happiest life. I once knew a young subaltern who had an account presented to him by the cashier of the firm of Peake and Allen, of the great continent of India, for nearly 300 rupees; and the items in said account were entirely chloric ether, extract of cardamoms —with the other component parts of a high-class restorative, and interest. Saddening! The next thing to avoid, the first thing in the morning, is soda-water, whether diluted with brandy or whisky. The "peg" may be all very well as an occasional potation, but, believe one who has tried most compounds, 'tis a precious poor "livener." On the contrary, although a beaker of the straw-coloured (or occasionally, mahogany-coloured) fluid may seem to steady the nerves for the time being, that effect is by no means lasting.

But the same panacea will not do in every case. If the patient be sufficiently convalescent to digest a

Doctor

(I do *not* mean a M.R.C.S.) his state must be far from hopeless. A "Doctor" is a mixture of beaten raw egg—not forgetting the white, which is of even more value than the yolk to the invalid—brandy, a little sifted sugar, and new milk. But many devotees of Bacchus could as soon swallow rum-and-oysters, in bed. And do not let us blame Bacchus unduly for the matutinal trouble. The fairy *Ala* has probably had a lot to do with that trouble. A "Doctor" can be made with sherry or whisky, instead of brandy; and many stockbrokers' clerks, sporting journalists, and other millionaires prefer a

Surgeon-Major,

who appears in the form of a large tumbler containing a couple of eggs beaten, and filled to the brim with the wine of the champagne district.

A Scorcher

is made with the juice of half a lemon squeezed into a large wine-glass; add a liqueur-glassful of old brandy, or Hollands, and a dust of cayenne. Mix well, and do not allow any lemon-pips to remain in the glass.

Prairie Oyster.

This is an American importation. There is a legend to the effect that one of a hunting party fell sick unto death, on the boundless prairie of Texas, and clamoured for oysters. Now the close and cautious bivalve no more thrives in a blue grass country than he possesses the ability to walk up stairs, or make a starting-price book. So one of the party, an inventive genius, cudgelled his brains for a substitute. He found some prairie hen's eggs, and administered the unbroken yolks thereof, one at a time, in a wine-glass containing a teaspoonful of vinegar. He shook the pepper-castor over the yolks and added a pinch of salt. The patient recovered. The march of science has improved on this recipe. Instead of despoiling the prairie hen, the epicure now looks to Madame Gobble for a turkey egg. And a

Worcester Oyster

is turned out ready made, by simply substituting a teaspoonful of Lea and Perrins' most excellent sauce for vinegar.

Brazil Relish.

This is, I am assured, a much-admired restorative in Brazil, and the regions bordering on the River Plate. It does not sound exactly the sort of stimulant to take after a "bump supper," or a "Kaffir" entertainment, but here it is: Into a wine-glass half full of curaçoa pop the unbroken yolk of a bantam's egg. Fill the glass up with maraschino. According to my notion, a good cup of hot, strong tea would be equally effectual, as an emetic, and withal cheaper. But they certainly take the mixture as a pick-me-up in Brazil.

Port-flip

is a favourite stimulant with our American cousins. Beat up an egg in a tumbler—if you have no metal vessels to shake it in, the shortest way is to put a clean white card, or a saucer, over the mouth of the tumbler, and shake —then add a little sugar, a glass of port, and some pounded ice. Strain before drinking. Leaving out the ice and the straining, this is exactly the same "refresher" which the friends of a criminal, who had served his term of incarceration in one of H.M. gaols, were in the habit of providing for him; and when the Cold Bath Fields Prison was a going concern, there was a small hostelry hard by, in which, on a Monday morning, the consumption of port wine (fruity) and eggs ("shop 'uns," every one) was considerable. This on the word of an ex-warder, who subsequently became a stage-door keeper.

One of the most unsatisfactory effects of good living is that the demon invoked over-night does not always assume the same shape in your waking hours. Many sufferers will feel a loathing for any sort of food or drink, except cold water. "The capting," observed the soldier-servant to a visitor (this is an old story), "ain't very well this morning, sir; he've just drunk his bath, and gone to bed again." And on the other hand, I have known the over-indulger absolutely ravenous for his breakfast. "Brandy and soda, no, dear old chappie; as many eggs as they can poach in five minutes, a thick rasher of York ham, two muffins, and about a gallon and a half of hot coffee—that's what I feel like." Medical men will be able to explain those symptoms in the roysterer, who had probably eaten and drunk quite as much over-night as the "capting." For the roysterer with a shy appetite there are few things more valuable than an

Anchovy Toast.

The concoction of this belongs to bedroom cookery, unless the sitting-room adjoins the sleeping apartment. For the patient will probably be too faint of heart to wish to meet his fellow-men and women downstairs, so early. The mixture must be made *over hot water*. Nearly fill a slop-basin with the boiling element, and place a soup-plate over it. In the plate melt a pat of butter the size of a walnut. Then having beaten up a raw egg, stir it in. When thoroughly incorporated with the butter add a dessert-spoonful of essence of anchovies. Cayenne *ad lib*. Then let delicately-browned crisp toast be brought, hot from the fire. Soak this in the mixture, and eat as quickly as you can. The above proportions must be increased if more than one patient clamours for anchovy toast; and this recipe is of no use for a dinner, or luncheon toast; remember that. After the meal is finished turn in between the sheets again for an hour; then order a "Doctor," or a "Surgeon-Major" to be brought to the bedside. In another twenty minutes the patient will be ready for his tub (with the chill off, if he be past thirty, and has any wisdom, or liver, left within him). After dressing, if he live in London and there be any trace of brain-rack remaining, let him take a brisk walk to his hair-dresser's, having his boots cleaned *en route*. This is most important, whether they be clean or dirty; for the action of a pair of briskly-directed brushes over the feet will often remove the most distressing of headaches. Arrived at the perruquier's, let the patient direct him to rub *eau de Cologne*, or some other perfumed spirit, into the o'er-taxed cranium, and to squirt assorted essences over the distorted countenance. A good hard brush, and a dab of bay rum on the temples will complete the cure; the roysterer will then be ready to face his employer, or the maiden aunt from whom he may have expectations.

If the flavour of the anchovy be disagreeable, let the patient try the following toast, which is similar to that used with wildfowl: Melt a pat of butter over hot water, stir in a dessert-spoonful of Worcester sauce, the same quantity of orange juice, a pinch of cayenne, and about half a wine-glassful of old port. Soak the toast in this mixture. The virtues of old port as a restorative cannot be too widely known.

St. Mark's Pick-me-up.

The following recipe was given to the writer by a member of an old Venetian family.

Ten drops of Angostura in a liqueur-glass, filled up with orange bitters. One wine-glassful of old brandy, one ditto cold water, one liqueur-glassful of curaçoa, and the juice of half a lemon. Mix well together. I have not yet tried this, which reads rather acid.

For an

Overtrained

athlete, who may not take kindly to his rations, there is no better cure than the lean of an underdone chop (*not blue* inside) hot from the fire, on a hot plate, with a glass of port poured over. A

Hot-pickle Sandwich

should be made of two thin slices of crisp toast (no butter) with chopped West Indian pickles in between. And for a

Devilled Biscuit

select the plain cheese biscuit, heat in the oven, and then spread over it a paste composed of finely-pounded lobster worked up with butter, made mustard, ground ginger, cayenne, salt, chili vinegar, and (if liked) a little curry powder. Reheat the biscuit for a minute or two, and then deal with it. Both the last-named restoratives will be found valuable (?) liver tonics; and to save future worry the patient had better calculate, at the same time, the amount of Estate Duty which will have to be paid out of his personalty, and secure a nice dry corner, out of the draught, for his place of sepulture. A

Working-Man's Livener,

(and by "working-man" the gentleman whose work consists principally in debating in taverns is intended) is usually a hair of the dog that bit him over-night; and in some instances where doubt may exist as to the particular "tufter" of the pack which found the working-man out, the livener will be a miscellaneous one. For solid food, this brand of labourer will usually select an uncooked red-herring, which he will divide into swallow-portions with his clasp-knife, after borrowing the pepper-castor from the tavern counter. And as new rum mixed with four-penny ale occasionally enters into the over-night's programme of the horny-handed one, he is frequently very thirsty indeed before the hour of noon.

I have seen a journalist suck half a lemon, previously well besprinkled with cayenne, prior to commencing his matutinal "scratch." But rum and milk form, I believe, the favourite livener throughout the district which lies between the Adelphi Theatre and St. Paul's Cathedral. And, according to Doctor Edward Smith (the chief English authority on dietetics), rum and milk form the most powerful restorative known to science. With all due respect to Doctor Smith I am prepared to back another restorative, commonly known as "a small bottle"; which means a pint of champagne. I have prescribed this many a time, and seldom known it fail. In case of partial failure repeat the dose. A valuable if seldom-employed restorative is made with

Bovril

as one of the ingredients. Make half-a-pint of beef-tea in a tumbler with this extract. Put the tumbler in a refrigerator for an hour, then add a liqueur-glassful of old brandy, with just a dust of cayenne. This is one of the very best pick-me-ups known to the faculty.

www.ingramcontent.com/pod-product-compliance
Lightning Source LLC
Chambersburg PA
CBHW081727100526
44591CB00016B/2531